NEW DIRECTIONS FOR ADULT AND CONTINUING EDUCATION

Susan Imel, *Ohio State University*
EDITOR-IN-CHIEF

The *New* Update on Adult Learning Theory

Sharan B. Merriam
The University of Georgia, Athens

EDITOR

Number 89, Spring 2001

JOSSEY-BASS
San Francisco

THE NEW UPDATE ON ADULT LEARNING THEORY
Sharan B. Merriam (ed.)
New Directions for Adult and Continuing Education, no. 89
Susan Imel, Editor-in-Chief

Microfilm copies of issues and articles are available in 16mm and 35mm,
as well as microfiche in 105mm, through University Microfilms Inc., 300
North Zeeb Road, Ann Arbor, Michigan 48106-1346.

ISSN 1052-2891   ISBN 0-7879-5773-9

NEW DIRECTIONS FOR ADULT AND CONTINUING EDUCATION is part of The
Jossey-Bass Higher and Adult Education Series and is published quarterly
by Jossey-Bass, 350 Sansome Street, San Francisco, California 94104-
1342.

SUBSCRIPTIONS cost $59.00 for individuals and $114.00 for institutions,
agencies, and libraries.

EDITORIAL CORRESPONDENCE should be sent to the Editor-in-Chief,
Susan Imel, ERIC/ACVE, 1900 Kenny Road, Columbus, Ohio
43210-1090. E-mail: imel.1@osu.edu.

Cover photograph by Wernher Krutein/PHOTOVAULT © 1990.

www.josseybass.com

Printed in the United States of America on acid-free recycled paper con-
taining 100 percent recovered waste paper, of which at least 20 percent is
postconsumer waste.

CONTENTS

EDITOR'S NOTES

Adult learning is probably the most studied topic in adult education. The learner, the learning process, and the context of learning form the cornerstone of the field of adult education. Whether one is planning or administering programs or counseling adults, or is directly involved in the teaching-learning transaction, adult learning is at the heart of our practice. The more we know about adult learning, the more effective our practice in the classroom, in the workplace, or in our communities. The purpose of *The New Update on Adult Learning Theory* is to present some of the latest thinking on adult learning.

This volume of the New Directions For Adult and Continuing Education series is unique in that it is a second edition of the popular 1993 volume, *An Update on Adult Learning Theory*. In the eight years between volumes, we have seen some additions to well-established theories and frameworks and more development of some new ideas introduced or just hinted at in 1993. One thing has remained the same over the years, however, and that is the lack of a single explanation or theory of adult learning. And I suspect that we will never agree on one, all-encompassing theory; adult learning is far too complex, too personal, and at the same time, too context-bound for one theory. Rather, we have an everchanging mosaic, where old pieces are rearranged and new pieces are added. The *New Update* tries to capture the look of this mosaic at this point in time.

To that end, this volume provides an update on well-established theories, expands some of the theories introduced in the 1993 edition, and presents some cutting-edge, very new approaches to adult learning.

The first three chapters of the new update review contributions of the last decade to andragogy, self-directed learning, transformational learning and informal and incidental learning. In Chapter One, I give a brief, historical overview of the development of the knowledge base in adult learning, beginning in the 1920s with the publication of *Adult Learning* (Thorndike, Bregman, Tilton, and Woodyard, 1928) and continuing up to the introduction of andragogy and self-directed learning in the late 1960s. Most of the chapter is devoted to updating the reader about work in the 1990s on these two important, foundational models of adult learning.

Lisa Baumgartner's chapter on transformational learning summarizes the burgeoning empirical research base that is refining and extending the theory proposed by Mezirow in the late 1970s. No other area of adult learning in the past decade has seen as much attention as transformational learning.

Informal and incidental learning has always been part of the landscape of adult learning. Recently, more attention has been given to this type of learning, especially as it occurs in organizations. In Chapter Three, Victoria

NEW DIRECTIONS FOR ADULT AND CONTINUING EDUCATION, no. 89, Spring 2001   © Jossey-Bass, A Publishing Unit of John Wiley & Sons, Inc.

Marsick and Karen Watkins review developments in this area and present their recently revised model of informal and incidental learning.

In the next three chapters, each of which has a counterpart in the 1993 edition, authors take a fresh look at women's learning, situated cognition (or context-based learning), and critical and postmodern perspectives. In Chapter Four, Elisabeth Hayes considers whether generalizations about women as learners can be supported, and then argues that learning is related to the context in which it occurs, and that constructions of gender shape this context. Catherine Hansman's chapter on context-based adult learning further explores how learning is situated in a context that involves both "tools" and social interaction. Next, Deborah Kilgore explains how critical theory and postmodern perspectives on adult learning are helping us to consider the assumptions and systemic forces that shape the adult learning context and the teaching-learning transaction.

Chapters Seven, Eight, and Nine are new additions. Chapter Seven, by John Dirkx, explores the role of emotions, feelings, and the imagination in the learning process. He argues, and recent research would suggest, that it is through emotions and images that we make meaning of our experiences, and that significant learning has an emotional component.

Lilian Hill's chapter on the brain and consciousness can be seen as a parallel discussion to Dirkx's chapter on emotions and imagination. She explains the structure of the brain and how it relates to learning, memory, emotions, the mind, and consciousness. In Chapter Nine, Carolyn Clark takes us one step further off the beaten track with a discussion of two very new ways to think about learning. One is somatic or embodied learning, through which we come to understand (know) through our physical body; the other is narrative learning, or how we learn through processing our experiences in the form of stories.

In the closing chapter of this new update, I step back and, with reference to the ideas and perspectives of previous chapters, comment on how the decade of the 1990s has advanced our understanding of adult learning and speculate on what the future might hold.

Sharan B. Merriam
Editor

Reference

Thorndike, E. L., Bregman, E. O., Tilton, J. W., and Woodyard, E. *Adult Learning*. New York: Macmillan, 1928.

SHARAN B. MERRIAM is professor of adult education at The University of Georgia, Athens.

1

Andragogy and self-directed learning continue to be important to our present-day understanding of adult learning.

Andragogy and Self-Directed Learning: Pillars of Adult Learning Theory

Sharan B. Merriam

The central question of how adults learn has occupied the attention of scholars and practitioners since the founding of adult education as a professional field of practice in the 1920s. Some eighty years later, we have no single answer, no one theory or model of adult learning that explains all that we know about adult learners, the various contexts where learning takes place, and the process of learning itself.

What we do have is a mosaic of theories, models, sets of principles, and explanations that, combined, compose the knowledge base of adult learning. Two important pieces of that mosaic are andragogy and self-directed learning. Other chapters in this volume focus on some of the newer approaches to understanding learning; the purpose of this chapter is to revisit two of the foundational theories of adult learning with an eye to assessing their "staying power" as important components of our present-day understanding of adult learning.

Early Research on Adult Learning

While we have known for centuries that adults learn as part of their daily lives, it wasn't until the early decades of the twentieth century that learning was studied systematically. The question that framed much of the early research on adult learning was whether or not adults *could* learn. The first book to report the results of research on this topic, Thorndike, Bregman, Tilton, and Woodyard's *Adult Learning* (1928), was published just two years after the founding of adult education as a professional field of practice. Thorndike and others approached adult learning from a behavioral psychological perspective. That is, people were tested under timed conditions on various learning and memory tasks.

NEW DIRECTIONS FOR ADULT AND CONTINUING EDUCATION, no. 89, Spring 2001 © Jossey-Bass, A Publishing Unit of John Wiley & Sons, Inc.

Findings from much of the early research were a function of research design. Tests of older adults against young people under timed conditions made it appear that being younger meant being a better learner. Lorge (1944, 1947) later pointed out that adult test scores were related to previous education and skills, not to age per se. Since older adults had less formal education and less opportunity to develop test-taking skills, it only appeared that they were less-capable learners. Moreover, when Lorge focused on adults' ability to learn rather than on the speed or rate of learning (that is, when time pressure was removed), adults up to age seventy did as well as younger adults.

The development of intelligence tests also came during this period. As with learning tasks, students scored well when compared to adults, as did young adults when compared to older adults. As the measurement of intelligence became more complex, scores indicated declines on some subtests but not on others. Today it is recognized that adults score better on some aspects of intelligence as they age and worse on others, resulting in a fairly stable composite measure of intelligence until very old age (Schaie and Willis, 1986).

In addition to intelligence, other aspects of human learning such as problem solving and cognitive development have been the focus of study by educational psychologists since the 1950s. Much of this research has not differentiated adults from children. When adults are included as part of the sample, the emphasis has been on how advancing age influences the ability to recall, to process information, and to problem solve. Generalizations from this set of literature are difficult to make, as much of the research has been conducted in laboratories or other artificial settings, making its applicability to real-life situations questionable. Further, deficits and declines are often shown to be functions of noncognitive factors such as level of education, training, health, and speed of response (Merriam and Caffarella, 1999).

Until mid–twentieth century, adult educators relied on research in psychology and educational psychology for an understanding of adult learning. As described, this research was behavioristic in design, and often insights about adult learning were extrapolated from research with children or research that placed adults under the same conditions as children. But as part of the drive to differentiate adult education from other forms of education, adult educators began to consider whether adult learning could be distinguished from learning in childhood. A new inquiry drove this effort. The question of whether adults could learn was put to rest, and the new focus of what was different about adult learning emerged. Thus, the drive to professionalize, which included the need to develop a knowledge base unique to adult education, was the context in which two of the field's most important theory-building efforts—andragogy and self-directed learning—emerged.

Andragogy

In 1968, Malcolm Knowles proposed "a new label and a new technology" of adult learning to distinguish it from preadult schooling (p. 351). The

European concept of andragogy, which he defined as "the art and science of helping adults learn," was contrasted with pedagogy, the art and science of helping children learn (Knowles, 1980, p. 43). Andragogy became a rallying point for those trying to define the field of adult education as separate from other areas of education.

The five assumptions underlying andragogy describe the adult learner as someone who (1) has an independent self-concept and who can direct his or her own learning, (2) has accumulated a reservoir of life experiences that is a rich resource for learning, (3) has learning needs closely related to changing social roles, (4) is problem-centered and interested in immediate application of knowledge, and (5) is motivated to learn by internal rather than external factors. From these assumptions, Knowles proposed a program-planning model for designing, implementing, and evaluating educational experiences with adults. For example, with regard to the first assumption that as adults mature they become more independent and self-directing, Knowles suggested that the classroom climate should be one of "adultness," both physically and psychologically. In an "adult" classroom, adults "feel accepted, respected, and supported"; further, there exists "a spirit of mutuality between teachers and students as joint inquirers" (1980, p. 47). And because adults manage other aspects of their lives, they are capable of directing, or at least assisting in planning, their own learning.

The 1970s and early 1980s witnessed much writing, debate, and discussion about the validity of andragogy as a theory of adult learning. At first the main point of contention was whether andragogy could be considered a "theory" of adult learning. Davenport and Davenport (1985, p. 157), in their chronicle of the debate, note that andragogy has been classified "as a theory of adult education, theory of adult learning, theory of technology of adult learning, method of adult education, technique of adult education, and a set of assumptions." Hartree (1984) questioned whether there was a theory at all, suggesting that perhaps these were just principles of good practice, or descriptions of "what the adult learner *should* be like" (p. 205). Knowles himself came to concur that andragogy is less a theory of adult learning than "a model of assumptions about learning or a conceptual framework that serves as a basis for an emergent theory" (1989, p. 112).

The second area of criticism, ongoing to this day, is the extent to which the assumptions are characteristic of *adult* learners only. Some adults are highly dependent on a teacher for structure, while some children are independent, self-directed learners. The same is true for motivation; adults may be externally motivated to learn, as in attending training sessions to keep their job, for example, while children may be motivated by curiosity or the internal pleasure of learning. Even the most obvious assumption that adults have more and deeper life experiences may or may not function positively in a learning situation. Indeed, certain life experiences can act as barriers to learning (Merriam, Mott, and Lee, 1996). Further, children in certain situations may have a range of experiences qualitatively richer than some adults (Hanson, 1996).

That these assumptions were not necessarily true of all adults led Knowles himself to revise his thinking as to whether andragogy was just for adults and pedagogy just for children. Between 1970 and 1980 he moved from an andragogy versus pedagogy position to representing them on a continuum ranging from teacher-directed to student-directed learning. He acknowledged that both approaches are appropriate with children and adults, depending on the situation. For example, an adult who knows little or nothing about a topic will be more dependent on the teacher for direction; at the other extreme, children who are naturally curious and who are "very self-directing in their learning *outside of school* . . . could also be more self-directed in school" (Knowles, 1984, p. 13). This acknowledgment by Knowles resulted in andragogy being defined more by the learning situation than by the learner.

Focusing on the teaching-learning situation seems to be the position taken by Cyril Houle, Knowles's mentor and author of a number of books on adult education. For Houle (1996, pp. 29–30), "education is fundamentally the same wherever and whenever it occurs. It deals with such basic concerns as the nature of the learner, the goals sought, the social and physical milieu in which instruction occurs, and the techniques of learning or teaching used. These and other components may be combined in infinite ways. . . . Andragogy remains as the most learner-centered of all patterns of adult educational programming." What is significant, Houle writes, is that andragogy has alerted educators to the fact that they "should involve learners in as many aspects of their education as possible and in the creation of a climate in which they can most fruitfully learn" (p. 30).

The scholarship on andragogy since 1990 has taken two directions. Some have analyzed the origins of the concept or its usage in different parts of the world. Another group of scholars has critiqued andragogy for its lack of attention to the context in which learning occurs.

Science, Discipline, or Technology? The ongoing international discussion and research on the concept of andragogy serves as a touchstone in the continued effort to professionalize through the establishment of a scientific discipline. Henschke (1998), citing several others, makes a point that andragogy with its humanistic philosophical underpinnings is well suited to democratically oriented societies. He suggests that the term can be illuminated through an analysis of Hebrew words that expand "and are also antecedent to the emergence of" the term. Andragogy, informed by humanism and Hebraic language, could be defined as "a scientific discipline" that studies everything related to learning and teaching "which would bring adults to their full degree of humaneness" (Henschke, 1998, p. 8). In another example of this thrust, Pastuovic (1995) explores the problems inherent in forming a scientific system for adult education. He finds andragogy to be the technological application of psychological and sociological knowledge, and not in itself "a science of the system of adult education" (p. 289).

Dusan Savicevic, who introduced Knowles to the term andragogy, has compared the concept in Europe and America. Andragogy originated in nineteenth-century Germany, where the educational programs of the workers' movement sought to differentiate themselves from children and schooling (Savicevic, 1998). In the second half of the twentieth century, andragogy was connected with the professionalization of adult education in both Europe and America. Out of the move to professionalize, as many as five conceptions of andragogy can be identified (Savicevic, 1991). For example, in some Central and Eastern European countries, where "pedagogy is an integrating science of education," andragogy is one of the disciplines of pedagogy (Savicevic, 1991, p. 197); in other countries andragogy and pedagogy are subsumed under the general science of education, and in yet other countries, andragogy is considered an independent scientific discipline.

Today the term andragogy is used in Poland, Germany, the Netherlands, Czechoslovakia, Russia, Yugoslavia, and other central and eastern European countries to refer to what the British and Americans call adult education (Draper, 1998). That is, andragogy as it has evolved in Europe is equivalent to our North American understanding of adult education as a professional field of practice (of which andragogy is but one prescriptive model of "how teachers and students should behave" [Savicevic, 1991, p. 198]). Even with these differences, Savicevic points out that both usages have several elements in common: roots in European culture; a "philosophy of lifelong education in which education and learning of adults is of primary importance"; increasing professionalism where andragogy, "under different names, has found its place in universities" as a discipline; and the emergence of professional organizations and publications (1998, p. 116). At the heart of the enterprise, whether it's called andragogy or adult education, is "the understanding of the position of a grown person in the process of education" (p. 114).

Context-Free Andragogy? The second stream of work in the 1990s has been a critique of the psychological focus of North American andragogy (Grace, 1996; Little, 1994; Pearson and Podeschi, 1997; Pratt, 1993). In the 1993 edition of *Update on Adult Learning Theory*, Pratt predicted that scholarship on andragogy would be characterized by the "tension between human agency and social structures as the most potent influences on adult learning. Here, andragogy is unconditionally on the side of human agency and the power of the individual to shed the shackles of history and circumstance in pursuit of learning" (p. 22).

Based in humanistic psychology, Knowles's version of andragogy presents the individual learner as one who is autonomous, free, and growth-oriented. Critics have pointed out that there is little or no acknowledgment that every person has been shaped by his or her culture and society, that every person has a history, and that social institutions and structures define, to a large extent, the learning transaction irrespective of the individual learner. Grace (1996, p. 383) notes that andragogy was introduced into North America in the late 1960s, "when action-oriented curricula that valued individual experience were advocated. The individual had to keep up and self-improvement was in *vogue*." And even though Knowles promoted andragogy for the next thirty years, he never considered "the organizational and social impediments to adult learning; he never painted the 'big picture.' He chose the mechanistic over the meaningful" (Grace, 1996, p. 386). Grace predicts that because "Knowles has reduced the adult learner to a technically proficient droid, operating in a world where formulaic social planning and self-directed learning mantras are the order of the day," he "is in danger of being left behind" (p. 391).

Discussions of andragogy in the decade of the 1990s demonstrate both its usefulness for exploring some of the definitional and philosophical issues related to the evolution of adult education as a scientific discipline, and its strengths and weaknesses as a guide to practice. And it is as a guide to practice that andragogy has had its biggest impact. As Pratt (1993, p. 21) in his assessment of andragogy writes, "andragogy has been adopted by legions of adult educators around the world. . . . Very likely, it will continue to be the window through which adult educators take their first look into the world of adult education." However, "while andragogy may have contributed to our understanding of adults as learners, it has done little to expand or clarify our understanding of the process of learning," nor has it achieved the status of "a theory of adult learning"(Pratt, 1993, p. 21).

Self-Directed Learning (SDL)

About the same time that Knowles introduced andragogy to North American adult educators, self-directed learning appeared as another model that helped define adult learners as different from children. Knowles (1975) himself contributed to the self-directed learning literature with a book explaining the concept and outlining how to implement it through learning contracts. And it might be recalled that the first assumption underlying Knowles's view of andragogy is that learners become increasingly self-directed as they mature. However, it was Tough (1967, 1971), building on the work of Houle (1961), who provided the first comprehensive description of self-directed learning as a form of study. Tough studied and described the self-planned learning projects of sixty-six Canadians. The uncovering and documenting of this type of learning—learning that is widespread, that occurs as part of adults' everyday life, and that is systematic yet does not depend on an instructor or a classroom—generated one of the major thrusts of research in the field of adult education.

Based on the pioneering work of Houle, Tough, and Knowles, early research in self-directed learning was descriptive, verifying the widespread presence of self-directed learning among adults and documenting the process by which it occurred. Overlapping with descriptive research, and continuing today, is work on model-building, discussions of the goals and ethics of SDL, clarifications of the nature of self-direction, and ways of assessing self-direction in learning. I will first summarize the literature according to the three categories presented in Merriam and Caffarella's 1999 review—the goals, the process, and the learner. This section is followed by an appraisal of the current status of self-directed learning research.

The Goals, the Process, the Learner. Depending on the philosophical orientation of the writer, the goals of self-directed leaning vary. Those grounded in a humanistic philosophy posit that self-directed learning should have as its goal the development of the learner's capacity to be self-directed. Knowles and Tough wrote from this perspective as do Brockett and Hiemstra (1991). In their Personal Responsibility Orientation (PRO) model of self-directed learning, human nature that is "basically good . . . accepting responsibility for one's own learning" and being proactive drive their model (p. 26).

A second goal is the fostering of transformational learning (Brookfield, 1986, Mezirow, 1985). Transformational learning as presented by Mezirow (see Chapter Two) posits critical reflection by the learner as central to the process (2000). This critical reflection is an "understanding of the historical, cultural, and biographical reasons for one's needs, wants, and interests. . . . Such self-knowledge is a prerequisite for autonomy in self-directed learning" (Mezirow, 1985, p. 27). Further, it is our job as adult educators "to assist adults to learn in a way that enhances their capability to function as self-directed learners" (Mezirow, 1981, p. 137).

The third goal for self-directed learning is the promotion of emancipatory learning and social action. Just as andragogy has been critiqued for ignoring the context of learning, so too some writers would like to see self-directed learning positioned more for social and political action than individual learning. Both Brookfield (1993) and Collins (1996) call for a more critical, political analysis of SDL. An example of this orientation is a recent study by Andruske (2000), wherein she investigated the self-directed learning projects of women on welfare. She found that the women became "political change agents as they attempt[ed] to control and to initiate change in their everyday worlds in response to oppressive external structures" (p. 11).

How one actually works through a self-directed learning experience has generated a number of models of the process. The earliest models proposed by Tough (1971) and Knowles (1975) are the most linear, moving from diagnosing needs to identifying resources and instructional formats to evaluating outcomes. Models developed in the late 1980s and the 1990s are less linear and more interactive; in such models not only the learner but the context of the learning and the nature of the learning itself are taken into account. In Danis's (1992) model, for example, learning strategies, phases of the learning process, the content, the learner, and the environmental factors in the context must all be taken into account in mapping the process of SDL.

What Merriam and Caffarella (1999) term "instructional" models of the process focus on what instructors can do in the formal classroom setting to foster self-direction and student control of learning. The best known of these is Grow's (1991, 1994) Staged Self-Directed Learning (SSDL) model. Grow presents a matrix whereby learners can locate themselves in terms of their readiness for and comfort with being self-directed, and instructors can match the learner's stage with appropriate instructional strategies. For example, whereas a dependent learner needs more introductory material and appreciates lecture, drill, and immediate correction, a self-directed learner can engage in independent projects, student-directed discussions, and discovery learning.

In addition to goals and process, the literature can be categorized according to the learner and the extent to which self-directedness is an a priori personal characteristic and associated with other variables such as educational level, creativity, learning style, and so on. Two scales of self-directedness, one measuring readiness (Guglielmino, 1997), and one measuring personal characteristics (Oddi, 1986), have been used in a number of studies. In addition to these empirical studies, the relationship between autonomy and self-directedness has been explored. Candy (1991, p. 309) writes that since a learner's autonomy is likely to "vary from situation to situation," educators should not assume that because a person has been self-directed in one situation, "he or she will be able to succeed in a new area: Orientation, support and guidance may all be required in the first stages of a learning project."

Current Assessment of SDL. The preceding brief overview of self-directed learning draws from a very broad literature base. Contributing to the literature has been fourteen years of meetings of the annual International Symposium on Self-Directed Learning. As the continuing existence of this conference attests, self-directed learning remains a viable arena for theory building related to adult learning. However, self-directed learning appears to be at a juncture in terms of *which* direction research and theory building should take in order to advance our understanding of this important dimension of adult learning. In an attempt to address this issue, Brockett et al. (2000) conducted a content analysis of 122 articles on self-directed learning published in fourteen periodicals between 1980 and 1998. They found that there has been a steady decline in the number of articles on SDL since the mid-1980s. Brockett (2000, p. 543) comments that this indicator, along with the shift away from "the individual adult learner toward looking at the sociopolitical context of adult education," might suggest that SDL has no future as a means for understanding adult learning. However, he makes the case that rather than move away from thirty years of scholarship on SDL, "the real challenge . . . is how to take the study of self-direction to a new level" (p. 543). The development of another instrument, a focus on the quality of the experience, studying how people engage and manage their self-directed learning, and asking about the ethical use or misuse of SDL are suggestions for this new work (Brockett, personal communication, September 28, 2000). Merriam and Caffarella (1999) list the following areas for investigation, all of which could expand our understanding of adult learning through SDL:

- How some adults remain self-directed in their learning over long periods of time
- How the process changes as learners move from novice to expert in subject matter and learning strategies

- How issues of power and control interact with the use of SDL in formal settings
- Whether being self-directed as a learner has an impact on one's instructional and planning activities
- What the role is of public policy in SDL
- What the critical practice of SDL looks like in practice
- How contextual factors interact with the personal characteristics of self-directed learners

Clearly, there are numerous possibilities for how future research on self-directed learning might enrich adult education practice as well as contribute to theory in adult learning.

Conclusion

This chapter began by explaining the context in which andragogy and SDL emerged. Appearing at about the same time, andragogy and self-directed learning were the first two attempts by adult educators to define adult education as a unique field of practice, one that could be differentiated from learning in general and childhood education in particular. Ironically, both have been criticized for a blinding focus on the individual learner while ignoring the sociohistorical context in which it occurs. However, both andragogy and SDL have become so much a part of adult education's identity, and have had such an impact on practice, that relegating them to the status of historical artifact is inconceivable. And, as we've seen in this chapter, today's scholars in both andragogy and self-directed learning are grappling with the tough issues. A more likely scenario is that both of these "pillars" of adult learning theory will continue to engender debate, discussion, and research, and in so doing, further enrich our understanding of adult learning.

References

Andruske, C. L. "Self-Directed Learning as a Political Act: Learning Projects of Women on Welfare." Proceedings of the 41st Annual Adult Education Research Conference,Vancouver, British Columbia, 2000.

Brockett, R. B. "Is It Time to Move On? Reflections on a Research Agenda for Self-Directed Learning in the 21st Century." Proceedings of the 41st Annual Adult Education Research Conference, Vancouver, British Columbia, 2000.

Brockett, R. B., and Hiemstra, R. Self-Direction in Adult Learning: Perspectives on Theory, Research, and Practice. London and New York: Routledge, 1991.

Brockett, R. B., et al. "Two Decades of Literature on SDL: A Content Analysis." Paper presented at the 14th International SDL Symposium, Boynton Beach, Florida, 2000.

Brookfield, S. Understanding and Facilitating Adult Learning. San Francisco: Jossey-Bass, 1986.

Brookfield, S. "Self-Directed Learning, Political Clarity, and the Critical Practice of Adult Education." Adult Education Quarterly, 1993, 43(4), 227–242.

Candy, P. C. Self-Direction for Lifelong Learning. San Francisco: Jossey-Bass, 1991.

Collins, M. "On Contemporary Practice and Research: Self-Directed Learning to Critical Theory." In R. Edwards, A. Hanson, and P. Raggatt (eds.), *Boundaries of Adult Learning: Adult Learners, Education and Training.* New York: Routledge, 1996.

Danis, C. "A Unifying Framework for Data-Based Research into Adult Self-Directed Learning." In H. B. Long and others (eds.), *Self-Directed Learning: Application and Research.* Norman: Oklahoma Research Center for Continuing Professional and Higher Education, University of Oklahoma, 1992.

Davenport, J., and Davenport, J., "A Chronology and Analysis of the Andragogy Debate." *Adult Education Quarterly,* 1985, *35*(3), 152–159.

Draper, J. A. "The Metamorphoses of *Andragogy." The Canadian Journal for the Study of Adult Education,* 1998, *12*(1), 3–26.

Grace, A. P. "Taking a Critical Pose: Andragogy—Missing Links, Missing Values." *International Journal of Lifelong Education,* 1996, *15*(5), 382–392.

Grow, G. "Teaching Learners to Be Self-Directed: A Stage Approach." *Adult Education Quarterly,* 1991, *41*(3), 125–149.

Grow, G. "In Defense of the Staged Self-Directed Learning Model." *Adult Education Quarterly,* 1994, *44*(2), 109–114.

Guglielmino, L. M. "Reliability and Validity of the Self-Directed Learning Readiness Scale and the Learning Preference Assessment (LPA)." In H. B. Long and others (eds.), *Expanding Horizons in Self-Directed Learning.* Norman: Public Managers Center, University of Oklahoma, 1997.

Hanson, A. "The Search for a Separate Theory of Adult Learning: Does Anyone Really Need Andragogy?" In R. Edwards, A. Hanson, and P. Raggatt (eds.), *Boundaries of Adult Learning.* New York: Routledge, 1996.

Hartree, A. "Malcolm Knowles' Theory of Androgogy: A Critique." *International Journal of Lifelong Education,* 1984, *3*(3), 203–210.

Henschke, J. A. "Historical Antecedents Shaping Conceptions of Andragogy: A Comparison of Sources and Roots." Paper presented at the International Conference on Research in Comparative Andragogy, Radovljica, Slovenia, 1998.

Houle, C. O. *The Inquiring Mind.* Madison: University of Wisconsin Press, 1961.

Houle, C. O. *The Design of Education.*(2nd ed.) San Francisco: Jossey-Bass, 1996.

Knowles, M. S. "Andragogy, Not Pedagogy." *Adult Leadership,* 1968, *16*(10), 350–352, 386.

Knowles, M. S. *Self-Directed Learning.* New York: Association Press, 1975.

Knowles, M. S. *The Modern Practice of Adult Education: From Pedagogy to Androgogy.* (2nd ed.) New York: Cambridge Books, 1980.

Knowles, M. S. *The Adult Learner: A Neglected Species.* (3rd ed.) Houston: Gulf, 1984.

Knowles, M. S. *The Making of an Adult Educator.* San Francisco: Jossey-Bass, 1989.

Knowles, M. S., and Associates. *Andragogy in Action: Applying Modern Principles of Adult Learning.* San Francisco: Jossey-Bass, 1985.

Little, D. "Toward Recovering and Reconstructing Andragogy." In *Proceedings of the Adult Education Research Conference,* Knoxville: University of Tennessee, May, 1994.

Lorge, I. "Intellectual Changes During Maturity and Old Age," *Review of Educational Research,* 1944, *14*(4), 438–443.

Lorge, I. "Intellectual Changes During Maturity and Old Age," *Review of Educational Research,* 1947, *17*(5), 326–330.

Merriam, S. B., and Caffarella, R. S. *Learning in Adulthood* (2nd ed.), San Francisco: Jossey-Bass, 1999.

Merriam, S. B., Mott, V. W., and Lee, M. "Learning That Comes from the Negative Interpretation of Life Experience." *Studies in Continuing Education,* 1996, *18*(1), 1–23.

Mezirow, J. "A Critical Theory of Adult Learning and Education." *Adult Education,* 1981, *32*(1), 3–27.

Mezirow, J. "A Critical Theory of Self-Directed Learning." In S. Brookfield (ed.), *Self-Directed Learning: From Theory to Practice.* New Directions for Continuing Education, no. 25. San Francisco: Jossey-Bass, 1985.

Mezirow, J., and Associates. *Learning as Transformation: Critical Perspectives on a Theory in Progress.* San Francisco: Jossey-Bass, 2000.

Oddi, L. F. "Development and Validation of an Instrument to Identify Self-Directed Continuing Learners." *Adult Education Quarterly,* 1986, *36*(2), 97–107.

Pastuovic, N. "The Science(s) of Adult Education." *International Journal of Lifelong Education,* 1995, *14*(4), 273–291.

Pearson, E., and Podeschi, R. "Humanism and Individualism: Maslow and His Critics." *Proceedings of the Adult Education Research Conference,* no. 38, Stillwater: Oklahoma State University, May, 1997.

Pratt, D. D. "Andragogy After Twenty-Five Years." In S. B. Merriam (ed.), *Update on Adult Learning Theory.* New Directions for Adult and Continuing Education, no. 57, San Francisco: Jossey-Bass, 1993.

Savicevic, D. M. "Modern Conceptions of Andragogy: A European Framework." *Studies in the Education of Adults,* 1991, 23(2), 179–201.

Savicevic, D. M. "Understanding Andragogy in Europe and America: Comparing and Contrasting. In J. Reischmann, B. Michal, and J. Zoran (eds.), *Comparative Adult Education 1998: The Contribution of ISCAE to an Emerging Field of Study.* Ljubljan, Slovenia: Slovenian Institute for Adult Education, 1998.

Schaie, K. W., and Willis, S. L. *Adult Development and Aging.* (2nd ed.) Boston: Little, Brown, 1986.

Thorndike, E. L., Bregman, E. O., Tilton, J. W., and Woodyard, E. *Adult Learning.* New York: Macmillan, 1928.

Tough, A. *Learning Without a Teacher.* Educational Research Series, no. 3. Toronto: Ontario Institute for Studies in Education, 1967.

Tough, A. *The Adult's Learning Projects: A Fresh Approach to Theory and Practice in Adult Learning.* Toronto: Ontario Institute for Studies in Education, 1971.

SHARAN B. MERRIAM is professor of adult education at The University of Georgia, Athens.

2

Four philosophical approaches to transformational learning, recent developments in Mezirow's theory, and fostering transformational learning are discussed.

An Update on Transformational Learning

Lisa M. Baumgartner

The word "transformation" evokes the notion of profound physical or psychological changes. Visions of caterpillars emerging as butterflies and deathbed conversions are popular images of transformation. Perhaps because transformational learning incites such far-reaching changes, interest in the topic continues to grow. In 1998, 150 people attended the First National Conference on Transformational Learning (Weissner and Mezirow, 2000). The conference is now an annual, eagerly anticipated event. The nature of transformational learning theory and its continued development are topics examined in this chapter.

Informational Learning Versus Transformational Learning

Steve, a twenty-something, up-and-coming actor, was pursuing his career when he was diagnosed HIV-positive in 1984. After the initial shock of the diagnosis subsided, Steve learned more about the disease through conversations with doctors, discussions with other HIV-positive people, and various publications. After reflecting on his priorities, Steve gained a new appreciation for his family and his world and concluded that his life's purpose was not to pursue material goals but to help others. What mattered was living and loving in the present. His worldview was transformed (Courtenay, Merriam, and Reeves, 1998). Steve continued to make meaning of his disease as life-extending medications, developed in the mid-1990s, resulted in him shifting his orientation from the present to the future. He started planning to live instead of planning to die.

NEW DIRECTIONS FOR ADULT AND CONTINUING EDUCATION, no. 89, Spring 2001   © Jossey-Bass, A Publishing Unit of John Wiley & Sons, Inc.

Steve's continued need to make meaning of his disease demonstrates that learning is a lifelong process. Much of our learning is additive in nature. We add on to what we already know. For example, Steve began to learn about HIV/AIDS when he was diagnosed and augmented his knowledge by talking with others and reading HIV/AIDS publications. Kegan (2000) calls this "informational learning," which refers to "extend[ing] already established cognitive capacities into new terrain" (p. 48). This type of learning "changes . . . *what* we know" (emphasis in the original) (p. 49).

In contrast, transformational learning, which can occur gradually or from a sudden, powerful experience, changes the way people see themselves and their world (Clark, 1993). Kegan (2000) says, "Literally, trans*form*-itive learning puts the form itself at risk of change (and not just change but increased capacity)" (p. 49, emphasis in the original). For example, prior to being diagnosed HIV-positive, Steve's career goal was to be a great actor. After diagnosis, it became more important to help others. Because his worldview changed, Steve valued serving others more than his own career advancement. In sum, while much of the learning that we do in adulthood is adding to *what* we know there is also the type of learning—transformational learning—that "changes . . . *how* we know" (Kegan, 2000, p. 49, emphasis in original).

Transformational Learning: A Four-Lens Approach

Transformational learning theory has been conceptualized several ways (Clark, 1993; Dirkx, 1998; Elias, 2000). Dirkx's four-lens approach provides a useful way to think about these unique transformational learning philosophies. One lens draws from Freire's (2000) notions of emancipatory education. Freire's work with the poor illiterate of Brazil helped him realize that the "banking method" of education, which emphasizes passive listening and acceptance of facts, kept his students disenfranchised (p. 53). Believing that education was for the purpose of liberation, Freire had students discuss and reflect on relevant life issues such as the inadequate pay they received as rural workers. Through this process, workers recognized the larger societal structures that oppressed them, and how they could overcome these barriers. Through consciousness-raising, or "conscientization" (p. 17), learners came to see the world and their place in it differently. Empowered in their new perspective, they could act to transform their world.

The cognitive-rational approach to transformational learning, advanced by Mezirow (1991; 2000), shares theoretical underpinnings with Freire. Both perspectives assert that adult education should lead to empowerment (Freire, 2000; Mezirow, 2000). Second, both take a constructivist approach to transformational learning. In short, knowledge is not "out there" to be discovered but is created from interpretations and reinterpretations in light of new experiences (Mezirow, 1996). The revised meaning results in what Mezirow calls a "perspective transformation," which is characterized by a "more inclusive, discriminating, permeable, and integrative perspective" (Mezirow, 1990, p. 14).

While Freire's focus is social-justice oriented, Mezirow concentrates on the importance of rational thought and reflection in the transformative learning process. Several fundamental components make up the recursive process that Mezirow delineates for perspective transformation. The process begins with a "disorienting dilemma" (Mezirow, 1991, p. 168), which is often a personal crisis such as Steve's HIV-positive diagnosis. Next, people engage in critical reflection and reevaluate the assumptions they have made about themselves and their world. This happens when people "realize something is not consistent with what [they] hold to be true" (Taylor, 1998, p. 9). Reflections on their meaning perspectives or their overarching "structure of assumptions" or their meaning schemes, which include their beliefs and values or "habitual, implicit *rules* for interpreting experience," can result in a perspective transformation or change in world view (Mezirow, 2000, p. 2, emphasis in the original). Third, people engage in "reflective discourse" (Mezirow, 2000, p. 11). In short, they talk with others about their new perspective to obtain consensual validation. Finally, action on the new perspective is imperative. In other words, not only *seeing*, but *living* the new perspective is necessary.

Long criticized for ignoring the affective, emotional, and social context aspects of the learning process (Clark and Wilson, 1991; Lucas, 1994; McDonald, Cervero, and Courtenay, 1999; Taylor, 1994), Mezirow in his most recent work (2000) acknowledges their importance in the meaning-making process. Learning occurs "in the real world in complex institutional, interpersonal, and historical settings [and] must be understood in the context of cultural orientations embodied in our frames of reference" (p. 24). He realizes that there are "asymmetrical power relationships" that influence the learning process (p. 28). Last, Mezirow acknowledges that social interaction is important in the learning relationship.

The developmental approach to transformational learning, the third lens, is most prominently articulated in Daloz's writings (1986; 1999). A college teacher and administrator, Daloz examines the interplay between education and development and realizes that students often are in a developmental transition and that they look to education to "help them make sense of lives whose fabric of meaning has gone frayed" (1999, p. 4). The transformational learning process is intuitive, holistic, and contextually based. It is a mythical procedure during which a mentor guides students in a learning journey affected by the student's social environment, including family dynamics and social class. Daloz's narrative approach to transformative learning humanizes the transformational learning process as he shares stories of students' struggles. These tales demonstrate how students negotiate developmental transitions and are changed in the process.

A fourth approach champions the link between spirituality and learning (Dirkx, 1997, 1998; Healy, 2000). Both Dirkx and Healy make a case for transformational learning having a spiritual dimension. Dirkx (1998) speaks of the role of imagination in facilitating learning through the soul and says that transformative learning goes beyond the ego-based, rational approach that relies on words to communicate ideas to an extrarational, soul-based learning that emphasizes feelings and images. Healy (2000) investigated the transformational learning process of those who practice insight meditation. He found respondents had an expanded self-awareness that simultaneously led to a deeper self-understanding and mindfulness in the present.

According to Taylor (1998), Mezirow believes resolution of "cognitive conflicts" leads to transformation, while the spiritual view recognizes that resolving intrapsychic conflicts is the key (p. 13). Further, knowledge comes not through critical reflection but through symbols (Dirkx, 1998). Transformation is an *extrarational* process that involves the integration of various aspects of the Self.

In sum, the emancipatory view of transformation, seen in Freire's work, acknowledges social inequities and champions liberation. In contrast, Mezirow, while recognizing the importance of the social context, concentrates on the cognitive aspects of the process including critical reflection and discussion. The developmental approach sees meaning-making as fundamental to being human and explicitly acknowledges the importance of mentors in the transformational learning process. Finally, the spiritual-integrative approach emphasizes the extrarational in transformative learning.

How We See Transformational Learning Now

Mezirow's conceptualization of transformational learning has generated the majority of the empirical research. In critical reviews of this research, Taylor (1997; 1998; 2000a; 2000b) has identified several ways the theory has been expanded. Following a review of Taylor's observations, three recent areas of inquiry will be investigated, including organizational or group transformations, fostering transformational learning, and the ethical considerations of facilitating a transformational learning experience.

Mezirow's Theory Expanded. The transformational learning journey was originally conceptualized as a linear process (Mezirow, as cited in Taylor, 2000b). However, further research indicates that it is "more individualistic, fluid, and recursive, than originally thought" (p. 292). In addition, certain *aspects* of the process, such as working through feelings, "seem to be more significant to change than [other aspects]" (p. 292). Taylor reports, "without the expression and recognition of feelings participants will not . . . begin critical reflection" (p. 291). In other words, transformational learning is a complex process involving thoughts and feelings.

Second, the triggering event or disorienting dilemma, which was originally conceptualized as a single, dramatic happening, may actually be a "long cumulative process" (Taylor, 2000b, p. 300). Taylor cites Clark's

(1991) research, which found that *several* events may converge to start the process. One participant, for example, began her journey toward feminism by taking a graduate course on the subject.

Third, Taylor (2000b) noted that "the importance of relationships" in the transformational learning process "was the most common finding among all the studies reviewed" (p. 307). Studies found that relational or rational discourse was "not only rationally driven but equally dependent on relational ways of knowing" (p. 306). In short, transformational learning is not an independent act but is an interdependent relationship built on trust.

Context and culture in the transformational learning process also seem to be more important than originally thought (Taylor, 2000b). Research has revealed that "personal contextual factors" such as a "readiness for change" make people predisposed to a transformational learning experience (p. 309). Research concerning "transformative learning in relation to difference" is scant, however (p. 310). Taylor cites Herber's (1998) study as an example of a study that investigated transformational learning and cultural difference. Specifically, Herber "explored whether transformative learning of preservice teachers could be precipitated by direct contact with historical records . . . of the African American civil rights movement." She found that contact with historical records was less a disorienting dilemma for African American students than it was a time for further integration (as cited in Taylor, 2000b, p. 311).

Groups and Organizational Transformational Learning. While most studies have been on individual transformation, recently an examination of group and organizational transformations has been a subject of inquiry (Davis and Ziegler, 2000; Kasl and Elias, 2000; Shaw and Taylor, 2000; Yorks and Marsick, 2000). Yorks and Marsick (2000) state that the goal of transformational organizational learning is for the organization to "realize its performance objectives" (p. 254). The authors report on two group learning strategies: action learning and collaborative inquiry. Both methods involve action and reflection. In action learning, people are placed on teams and asked to solve a problem or issue. Through extensive reflection and dialogue they work at a solution. This method produced sustained changes in the organizational culture (Yorks and Marsick, 2000).

Unlike action learning, collaborative inquiry (CI) invites voluntary participation and the question of interest "is framed by the group with no outside interference" (Yorks and Marsick, 2000, p. 266). In this study, six faculty or staff members asked the question, "How can we help students take more responsibility for their own learning in a way which makes the university more of a learning organization?" (p. 267). A freshman cohort was created that took the professors' classes together. This new structure provided opportunities for faculty to learn individually as well as for organizational learning to occur. "Faculty clusters" met as a team to "create learning links among the courses" (p. 269) and in the process their teaching practices were transformed.

Kasl and Elias (2000) report on the transformational learning that occurred in an organizational change effort. This tale of transformation describes "changes in the structure . . . and the content of the group's consciousness" (p. 234). Specifically, it delineates how the group adjusts to the new frames of reference as the school is reorganized, the critical reflection they engaged in to clarify their mission, and the new worldview that emerged. The importance of "discernment [and] critical reflection" in the process of finding a group identity is also articulated (p. 248). The authors state: "The group changed its premise about its identity first by elaborating its frame of reference for faculty, then by adding a new frame of learning community, and finally by transcending both of these identities and creating a new identity as a praxis collective" (p. 248).

Davis and Ziegler's (2000) study investigated a transformational change in the organizational culture of human services offices. In this study, welfare recipients' case workers and potential employers met to discuss a survey that outlined the "knowledge, skills, and attitudes" (p. 124) welfare recipients needed for employment. This collaboration led to partnerships between agencies and employers. Consequently, agencies saw themselves as places for job training and placement instead of organizations only interested in welfare compliance.

Fostering Transformative Learning. Recently, more has been written about fostering transformative learning (Gozawa, 2000; Lam and O'Neil, 2000; Meyer, 2000). Taylor (2000a) reviewed twenty-three studies that used Mezirow's model and focused on fostering transformational learning in the classroom. He found support for some of Mezirow's ideal conditions for transformational learning, including the need for "a safe, open, and trusting environment" that allows for participation, collaboration, exploration, critical reflection, and feedback (p. 154).

Cranton's (1994; 1996; 2000) writings focus on *how* to create Mezirow's ideal conditions in the classroom. She suggests instructors relinquish some of their authority or "position power" in the classroom (Cranton, 1994, p. 147). Using first names and having learning contracts are two ways to do this. Second, Cranton (1994; 2000) recommends recognizing learners' learning styles in order to help them critically question their assumptions. For example, those using logic may enjoy debate as a method to critically question their assumptions, while intuitive individuals may rely on hunches and images (Cranton, 2000).

Taylor's review (2000a) uncovers several ways to foster transformational learning in the classroom. First, "fostering group ownership and individual agency" promotes transformational learning (p. 155). Taylor cites Saavedra's (1995) study, which focused on the learning process of a teacher's group devoted to improving their instructional techniques. Taylor states that "placing teachers *at the center* of their own learning in a critically reflective and social group setting contributed to transformation" (p. 155). Second, studies revealed that teachers need to "capitalize on the interrelationship between critical reflection and affective learning" (p. 156). Taylor notes, "The significance of processing feelings increases the power and appreciation of critical reflection when fostering transformational learning" (p. 156). Finally, value-laden course content appeared to foster transformational learning in that discussions about controversial topics "provoked critical reflection . . . more so than other content" (p. 156).

Ethical Considerations in Transformational Learning. While fostering transformational learning has been a topic of interest, questions remain concerning the educator's role in planning a transformational learning experience and the educator's responsibility for its impact (Courtenay, Merriam, Reeves, and Baumgartner, 2000). What right do instructors have to encourage transformational learning?

While not directly addressing the ethics of instigating a transformational learning experience, Robertson (1996) recognizes that the teacher-learner relationship is one of trust and caring that is vital to creating the right conditions for a transformational learning experience. Realizing that most adult educators are unprepared to "manage the dynamics of helping relationships or the dynamics of transformative learning within the context of those relationships" (pp. 43–44), he makes several recommendations. First, the field must recognize a teacher-learner–centered approach instead of exclusively a learner-centered approach. Second, he recommends that more be authored on the dynamics of the teacher-learner relationship and that a "curriculum for adult educators . . . include[ing] managing the dynamics of educational helping relationships" be written (p. 48). Having a formal code of ethics has been a matter of debate (Carlson, 1988; Cunningham, 1992). Robertson (1996) sees advantages to the field of adult education having a code of ethics while acknowledging the value in continuing to reflect on and discuss ethics-related issues. Finally, adult educators need a forum in which to discuss "issues related to the dynamics of the helping relationship" (p. 49).

Differential power dynamics in the classroom also require sensitivity. Smith's (2000) study, which examined the experiences of university students between the ages of sixty-six and seventy-six, showed that older students saw the professor as an authority figure. The transformational learning process involves questioning, critical reflection, and the need to engage in "rational discourse" to gain consensual validation for a new perspective (Mezirow, 1991, p. 168). Students who see the professor as an authority figure may be unable or unwilling to question their teacher's values. Transformational learning is difficult to achieve in this setting. Ethics regarding the power differential arise. Cranton (1994) advises that teachers explicitly state their values and "model questioning their own values" (p. 201).

In sum, it is important to remember that the transformational learning process involves emotions. Whether or not instructors should intentionally plan for a transformative learning experience may still be a matter of debate. Whether planned or happenstance, new ideas may threaten students' worldviews.

Conclusion

Transformational learning theory has expanded our understanding of adult learning by explicating the meaning-making process. It is not *what* we know but *how* we know that is important. Philosophical approaches to transformational learning multiply as new research generates fresh ideas.

In particular, research using Mezirow's theory has yielded insights into the importance of relationships, feelings, and context in the process. Group and organizational transformation, fostering transformational learning, and the ethical considerations involved are current topics of interest. Critical reflection on the theory in combination with thoughtful discussion is leading to a broader, more inclusive understanding of transformational learning.

References

Carlson, R. A. "A Code of Ethics for Adult Educators?" In R. G. Brockett, (ed.), *Ethical Issues in Adult Education*. New York: Teachers College Press, 1988.

Clark, M. C. "The Restructuring of Meaning: An Analysis of the Impact of Context on Transformational Learning." Unpublished doctoral dissertation, Department of Adult Education, University of Georgia, 1991.

Clark, M. C. "Transformational Learning." In S. B. Merriam (ed.), *An Update on Learning Theory*. New Directions for Adult and Continuing Education, no. 57. San Francisco: Jossey-Bass, 1993.

Clark, M. C., and Wilson, A. L. "Context and Rationality in Mezirow's Theory of Transformational Learning." *Adult Education Quarterly*, 1991, *41*(2), 75–91.

Courtenay, B. C., Merriam, S. B., and Reeves, P. M. "The Centrality of Meaning-Making in Transformational Learning: How HIV-Positive Adults Make Sense of Their Lives." *Adult Education Quarterly*, 1998, *48*(2), 102–119.

Courtenay, B. C., Merriam, S. B., Reeves, P. M., and Baumgartner, L. M. "Perspective Transformation Over Time: A Two-Year Follow-Up Study of HIV-Positive Adults." *Adult Education Quarterly*, 2000, *50*(2), 102–119.

Cranton, P. *Understanding and Promoting Transformative Learning: A Guide for Educators of Adults*. San Francisco: Jossey-Bass, 1994.

Cranton, P. *Professional Development as Transformative Learning*. San Francisco: Jossey-Bass, 1996.

Cranton, P. "Individual Differences and Transformative Learning." In J. Mezirow and Associates (eds.), *Learning as Transformation: Rethinking Adult Learning and Development*. San Francisco: Jossey-Bass, 2000.

Cunningham, P. M. "Adults and Continuing Education Do Not Need a Code of Ethics." In M. W. Galbraith and B. R. Sisco (eds.), *Confronting Controversies in Challenging Times: A Call for Action*. New Directions for Adult and Continuing Education, no. 54, San Francisco: Jossey-Bass, 1992.

Daloz, L. A. *Effective Teaching and Mentoring: Realizing the Transformational Power of Adult Learning Experiences*. San Francisco: Jossey-Bass, 1986.

Daloz, L. A. *Mentor: Guiding the Journey of Adult Learners*. San Francisco: Jossey-Bass, 1999.

Davis, D. C., and Ziegler, M. F. "Transformative Learning at a Large-System Level: Using a Participative Research Process to Help Change the Culture of a State's Welfare System." In C. A. Wiessner, S. R. Meyer, and D. A. Fuller (eds.), *The Third International Transformative Learning Conference: Challenges of Practice: Transformative Learning in Action*. New York: Columbia University, 2000.

Dirkx, J. M. "Nurturing the Soul in Adult Learning." In P. Cranton (ed.), *Transformative Learning in Action: Insights from Practice*. New Directions for Adult and Continuing Education, no. 74. San Francisco: Jossey-Bass, 1997.

Dirkx, J. M. "Transformative Learning Theory in the Practice of Adult Education: An Overview." *PAACE Journal of Lifelong Learning*, 1998, 7, 1–14.

Elias, J. "One Strategy for Facilitating Transformative Learning: Synergic Inquiry." In C. A. Wiessner, S. R. Meyer, and D. A. Fuller (eds.), *The Third International Transformative Learning Conference: Challenges of Practice: Transformative Learning in Action*. New York: Columbia University, 2000.

Freire, P. *Pedagogy of the Oppressed*. (Revised 20th Anniversary Edition). New York: Continuum, 2000.

Gozawa, J. "Cosmic Heroes and the Heart's Desire: Embracing Emotion and Conflict in Transformational Learning." In C. A. Wiessner, S. R. Meyer, and D. A. Fuller (eds.), *The Third International Transformative Learning Conference: Challenges of Practice: Transformative Learning in Action*. New York: Columbia University, 2000.

Healy, M. "East Meets West: Transformational Learning and Buddhist Meditation." In T. Sork, V. Lee, and R. St. Claire (eds.), *AERC 2000 An International Conference: Proceedings from the 41st Annual Adult Education Research Conference*. Vancouver: University of British Columbia, 2000.

Herber, M. S. "Perspective Transformation in Preservice Teachers." Unpublished doctoral dissertation. University of Memphis, 1998.

Kasl, E., and Elias, D. "Transforming Systems: Creating New Habits of Mind in Small Groups." In J. Mezirow and Associates (eds.), *Learning as Transformation: Critical Perspectives on a Theory on Progress*. San Francisco: Jossey-Bass, 2000.

Kegan, R. "What 'Form' Transforms?: A Constructive-Developmental Perspective on Transformational Learning." In J. Mezirow and Associates (eds.), *Learning as Transformation: Critical Perspectives on a Theory in Progress*. San Francisco: Jossey-Bass, 2000.

Lam, S., and O'Neil, J. "Comparing the Learner's and Educator's Perspectives on Conditions That Foster Transformative Learning in Action Learning Programs." In C. A. Wiessner, S. R. Meyer, and D. A. Fuller (eds.), *The Third International Transformative Learning Conference: Challenges of Practice: Transformative Learning in Action*. New York: Columbia University, 2000.

Lucas, L. L. "The Role of Courage in Transformational Learning." Unpublished doctoral dissertation, University of Wisconsin, 1994.

McDonald, B., Cervero, R. M., and Courtenay, B. C. "An Ecological Perspective of Power in Transformational Learning: A Case Study of Ethical Vegans." *Adult Education Quarterly*, 1999, *50*(2), 5–23.

Meyer, S. R. "Journaling and Transformative Learning." In C. A. Wiessner, S. R. Meyer, and D. A. Fuller (eds.), *The Third International Transformative Learning Conference: Challenges of Practice: Transformative Learning in Action*. New York: Columbia University, 2000.

Mezirow, J. *Transformative Dimensions of Adult Learning*. San Francisco: Jossey-Bass, 1991.

Mezirow, J. "Contemporary Paradigms of Learning." *Adult Education Quarterly*, 1996, *46*(3), 158–172.

Mezirow, J. "Learning to Think Like an Adult: Transformation Theory: Core Concepts." In J. Mezirow and Associates (eds.) *Learning as Transformation: Critical Perspectives on a Theory in Progress*. San Francisco: Jossey-Bass, 2000.

Mezirow, J., and Associates. *Fostering Critical Reflection in Adulthood*. San Francisco: Jossey-Bass, 1990.

Robertson, D. "Facilitating Transformative Learning: Attending to the Dynamics of the Helping Relationship." *Adult Education Quarterly*, 1996, *47*(1), 41–53.

Saavedra, E. R. "Teacher Transformation: Creating Text and Contexts in Study Groups." Unpublished doctoral dissertation. Tucson: University of Arizona, 1995.

Shaw, M., and Taylor, L. "Leadership Development and Organizational Transformation." In C. A. Wiessner, S. R. Meyer, and D. A. Fuller (eds.), *The Third International Transformative Learning Conference: Challenges of Practice: Transformative Learning in Action.* New York: Columbia University, 2000.

Smith, B. "Learning Experiences of Older Adults as University Students: Opportunities for Transformational Learning." In C. A. Wiessner, S. R. Meyer, and D. A. Fuller (eds.), *The Third International Transformative Learning Conference: Challenges of Practice: Transformative Learning in Action.* New York: Columbia University, 2000.

Taylor, E. W. "Intercultural Competency: A Transformative Learning Process." *Adult Education Quarterly,* 1994, 44(3), 154–174.

Taylor, E. W. "Transformative Learning—A Review." *Adult Education Quarterly,* 1997, 48(1), 34–59.

Taylor, E. W. "The Theory and Practice of Transformative Learning: A Critical Review." ERIC Clearinghouse on Adult, Career and Vocational Education (Information Series No 374). Columbus, Ohio, 1998.

Taylor, E. W. "Fostering Transformational Learning in the Adult Education Classroom: A Review of the Empirical Studies." In C. A. Wiessner, S. R. Meyer, and D. A. Fuller (eds.), *The Third International Transformative Learning Conference: Challenges of Practice: Transformative Learning in Action.* New York: Columbia University, 2000a.

Taylor, E. W. "Analyzing Research on Transformative Learning Theory." In J. Mezirow and Associates (eds.), *Learning as Transformation: Critical Perspectives on a Theory in Progress.* San Francisco: Jossey-Bass, 2000b.

Weissner, C. A., and Mezirow, J. "Theory Building and the Search for Common Ground." In J. Mezirow and Associates (eds.), *Learning as Transformation: Critical Perspectives on a Theory in Progress.* San Francisco: Jossey-Bass, 2000.

Yorks, L., and Marsick, V. "Transformative Learning in Organizations." In J. Mezirow & Associates (eds.), *Learning as Transformation: Critical Perspectives on a Theory in Progress.* San Francisco: Jossey-Bass, 2000.

LISA M. BAUMGARTNER *is assistant professor of adult education at Buffalo State College, Buffalo, New York.*

3

This chapter provides a theory of informal and incidental learning and updates this theory based on recent research.

Informal and Incidental Learning

Victoria J. Marsick, Karen E. Watkins

Informal and incidental learning is at the heart of adult education because of its learner-centered focus and the lessons that can be learned from life experience. But learning from experience is so broad that everything from Outward Bound activities to structured computer simulations is included in the definition. In this chapter we define informal and incidental learning and look at questions that arise when adult educators use this type of learning in research and practice.

What Informal and Incidental Learning Look Like

We define informal and incidental learning by their contrast with formal learning:

> Formal learning is typically institutionally sponsored, classroom-based, and highly structured. Informal learning, a category that includes incidental learning, may occur in institutions, but it is not typically classroom-based or highly structured, and control of learning rests primarily in the hands of the learner. Incidental learning is defined as a byproduct of some other activity, such as task accomplishment, interpersonal interaction, sensing the organizational culture, trial-and-error experimentation, or even formal learning. Informal learning can be deliberately encouraged by an organization or it can take place despite an environment not highly conducive to learning. Incidental learning, on the other hand, almost always takes place although people are not always conscious of it [Marsick and Watkins, 1990, p. 12].

Informal learning is usually intentional but not highly structured. Examples include self-directed learning, networking, coaching, mentoring, and performance planning that includes opportunities to review learning needs. When people learn incidentally, their learning may be taken for granted, tacit, or unconscious. However, a passing insight can then be probed and intentionally explored. Examples are the hidden agenda of an organization's culture or a teacher's class, learning from mistakes, or the unsystematic process of trial and error.

The origins of our theory of informal and incidental learning have been reviewed by us (Marsick and Watkins, 1990) and by Garrick (1998). In these reviews, informal and incidental learning have been linked to related concepts, such as learning "en passant" (Reischmann, 1986), the distinctions several others have made between formal, informal, and nonformal learning (Coombs and Ahmed, 1974; Mocker and Spear, 1982; Jarvis, 1987), social modeling (Bandura, 1986), experiential learning (Boud, Cohen, and Walker, 1993; Kolb, 1984), self-directed learning (Candy, 1991; Knowles, 1950), action learning as a variant of experiential learning (Revans, 1982), action science (Argyris and Schön, 1974, 1978) and reflection in action (Schön, 1983), critical reflection and transformative learning (Mezirow, 1991), tacit knowing (Nonaka and Takeuchi, 1995; Polanyi, 1967), situated cognition (Scribner, 1986; Lave and Wenger, 1991), and communities of practice (Wenger, 1998). These concepts are related to informal and incidental learning, but they are not synonymous with the terms in the way that we use them here.

What We've Learned from Research

Mary Callahan (1999) identified almost 150 studies when doing her research on this topic. A review of this research makes it immediately clear that informal and incidental learning are relevant to practice in many cultures and contexts: the private and public sectors, hospitals and health care, colleges and universities, schools, professional associations, museums, religions, families, and communities.

Some specific studies illustrate how such knowledge enhances our learning. Dana Diesel and Elizabeth Colbert, doctoral students at Teachers College, Columbia University, are conducting a joint study in an experimental elementary school in North Carolina. Colbert is one of the school's leaders, but all administrators also teach and all teachers also participate in governance. Colbert and Diesel are studying how teachers learn informally through reflection and action and ways in which their collaboration is nurtured in the culture. In many schools, professional development for teachers is often limited to occasional, brief in-service sessions. The findings from this study can be used to design policies, practices, and a culture that supports ongoing learning that is integrated with daily work routines within the school.

Callahan (1999) studied incidental learning in a publicly funded small-business incubator. Business incubators support new entrepreneurial ventures by providing technical assistance, resources, and services. The incubator provided opportunities and a culture for informal observing and talking with others, particularly those who used the incubator's free office space with new ventures housed in the same space once occupied by now successful startups. Callahan's interviewees referred to one kind of incidental learning as the "karma in the walls and halls." Observing other start-up companies provided participants with "a virtual blueprint" to guide early entrepreneurial steps. "Bridging" learning helped people with different professional backgrounds (in this instance, technical entrepreneurs and venture capitalists) to understand one another and work more effectively together. By providing opportunities for interaction and sharing, adult educators built on the natural enthusiasm for learning of these technically-oriented entrepreneurs and moved them from learning about their technical innovations to learning about managing a business.

Maria Cseh's (1998) study found that the learning of the owner-managers of small, successful, private companies in Romania was stimulated mostly by the context, particularly the ambiguity, of a quasi–market economy. One of the major lessons learned by these owner-managers was that although there were many changes after the collapse of the Communist regime, little changed in the way human relationships in business were conducted. Thus, those managers who did not have managerial experience in the previous regime had to learn how to work with the government and state-owned companies, while those who had previous experience had difficulty unlearning previous politically-driven practices that only worked half of the time. Cseh's study poses questions for research and practice around the nature and facilitation of "unlearning." As illustrated by the Eastern European managers in this study, freeing oneself from existing mental models that constrain the way work is done is not easy.

Studies by Carter (1995) and Menard (1993) illustrate that informal and incidental learning are often the result of a significant unplanned or unexpected event. Carter studied stroke survivors whose newsletter title speaks to their surprise trigger to learning: "A Stroke of Luck." Her study found that stroke survivors more often than not had to figure out on their own a solution to the problems they encountered, despite health care systems that intended to be supportive. Menard's study looked at the informal and incidental learning of nurses in Vietnam. Numerous critical incidents identified the satisfaction the nurses found in their own ingenuity in inventing tools or techniques to accommodate for the lack of critical supplies in MASH units.

Finally, a study by Watkins and Cervero (2000) sought to determine whether two different organizational settings of CPA practice produced substantially different or equivalent learning opportunities for a practicing CPA. The study was conducted to provide expert testimony for a lawsuit. The CPA worked for approximately two-and-a-half years in a registered CPA firm, at which point he became an employee of a financial services firm that was not a registered CPA firm. The questions raised in the lawsuit had to do with the time needed in either environment for professional certification (labeled "experience credit" by CPAs–or time-learning-by-doing accounting). Watkins and Cervero constructed a survey of thirty-one possible formal, informal, and incidental learning opportunities. For example, they asked whether the CPA had opportunities to learn from instructional videos, from being assigned increasingly difficult accounting projects, and from critiquing sessions with supervisors. The new CPA participated in twenty-one out of the twenty-five learning opportunities available at both organizations. Learning was intricately woven into the fabric of work in both organizations. Watkins and Cervero concluded that there was a strong culture and support for learning at both organizations, and no substantial difference between the firms in the formal, informal, and incidental learning opportunities available.

Adult educators and organizations can learn from the structures and strategies supported by professional service firms and from the research presented briefly here. The organizational context produces different work assignments, which, in turn, lead to different opportunities and priorities for learning. The organization can provide different incentives for learning, such as tuition reimbursement, and resources, such as a library of reference material, subscriptions to professional journals, video courses, or computer-based courses. In particular, the organization can encourage peers to work and learn collaboratively (Marsick and Watkins, 1999; Watkins and Marsick, 1993, 1996).

Informal and incidental learning take place wherever people have the need, motivation, and opportunity for learning. After a review of several studies done on informal learning in the workplace, Marsick and Volpe (1999) concluded that informal learning can be characterized as follows:

- It is integrated with daily routines.
- It is triggered by an internal or external jolt.
- It is not highly conscious.
- It is haphazard and influenced by chance.
- It is an inductive process of reflection and action.
- It is linked to learning of others [p. 5].

Model for Enhancing Informal and Incidental Learning

Figure 3.1 depicts a model for enhancing informal and incidental learning that Marsick and Watkins developed initially in 1990 and have subsequently modified, most recently in collaboration with Cseh (Cseh, Watkins, and Marsick, 1999). The model is rooted in the thinking of John Dewey (1938), Argyris and Schön (1974, 1978), and Mezirow (1991).

Figure 3.1.   Marsick and Watkins's Informal and Incidental Learning Model as Adapted with Cseh

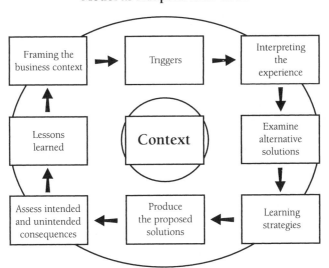

The circle in the center represents our belief that learning grows out of everyday encounters while working and living in a given context. A new life experience may offer a challenge, a problem to be resolved, or a vision of a future state. The outer circle represents the context within which the experience occurs, the personal, social, business, and cultural context for learning that plays a key role in influencing the way in which people interpret the situation, their choices, the actions they take, and the learning that is effected.

The model depicts a progression of meaning making that, in practice, is often more of an ebb and flow as people begin to make sense of a situation. With each new insight, they may have to go back and question earlier understandings. The model is arranged in a circle, but the steps are neither linear nor necessarily sequential.

In this newest version of our model, we have integrated the incidental learning process since it is clear to us that it is always occurring, with or without our conscious awareness. For example, we note that learning begins with some kind of a trigger, that is, an internal or external stimulus that signals dissatisfaction with current ways of thinking or being. This trigger or experience encountered is often a surprise, such as the sudden departure of a leader. But in the model, preceding this is our worldview, our way of seeing things that frames what we pay attention to, how we will see this new trigger. This frame is a pivotal point in the model since it can also be influenced by the lessons learned at the end of a learning cycle. Our model shows that people diagnose or frame a new experience that they encounter. They assess what is problematic or challenging about it. They compare the new situation with prior experience, identify similarities or differences, and use their interpretation to make sense of the new challenge.

People refine their diagnosis by interpreting the context. They attend to the different factors in the context that influence their interpretation. The context might simply involve one other person, say a family member or coworker, and a relatively routine interaction. Or it might be highly complex, with multiple actors and many political, social, or cultural norms that have never before been addressed. Interpreting the context is a greater challenge when social norms and expectations are in a state of flux, or when the person himself or herself is learning something new. Also, people do not have the same level of skill or awareness around contextual factors that influence an interpretation, and they are subject to blind spots that can, at times, be intensified when emotional factors come into play.

Interpretation of the context leads to choices about alternative actions. These choices are guided by recollections of past solutions and by a search for other potential models for action. Success in implementation depends on drawing on capabilities that are adequate to the task. If the solution calls for new skills, the person needs to acquire these. Many contextual factors influence the ability to learn well enough to successfully implement the desired solution. These include, but may not be limited to, the availability of appropriate resources (time, money, people from whom to learn, available knowledge about an unknown or ambiguous phenomena), willingness and motivation to learn, and the emotional capacity to take on new capabilities in the middle of what could be a stressful challenge.

Once an action is taken (a solution produced), a person can assess the outcomes and decide whether or not they match his or her goals, the intended results. It is relatively easy to assess intended consequences if a person takes the time up front to make his or her goals clear and explicit. This step of judging consequences then enables a person to draw lessons learned and to use these lessons in planning future actions. These concluding thoughts are the new understandings or frame that a person would bring when encountering a new situation, which brings us back full circle to the beginning of the cycle.

Implications for Practice: Enhancing Informal and Incidental Learning

Informal and incidental learning generally take place without much external facilitation or structure. In our work, we emphasize three conditions to enhance this kind of learning: critical reflection to surface tacit knowledge and beliefs, stimulation of proactivity on the part of the learner to actively identify options and to learn new skills to implement those options or solutions, and creativity to encourage a wider range of options.

Individuals who want to enhance this learning can increase their own awareness of the learning opportunities posed by life experiences and gain insight into their learning preferences. Adult educators might provide a structure within which to take advantage of learning opportunities and gain insight into oneself as learner. Honey and Mumford (1989), for example, provide guidelines for self-analysis of learning styles and for action planning around improved capability. Many organizations use learning-style instruments in career-planning workshops to encourage employees to become more self-directed in planning their careers and development. People learn how they learn, examine multiple ways to learn, and look for ways to more effectively plan their future learning to play to their learning preferences.

Adult educators can also help learners identify conditions in the socio-cultural context that help them learn more effectively or that stand in the way of learning. Once these factors are identified, educators can help learners change or deal with them. For example, a number of governments no longer provide indefinite welfare assistance to poor people and instead require them to work. Programs that prepare welfare recipients for getting and keeping work may not question the role that society has played in causing the conditions that create poverty or the discrimination that some people may experience due to their gender, race, or class. Poor welfare women may learn incidentally that they are to blame for many of their problems. When these women learn informally about work opportunities, they may seek socially sanctioned work paths that actually reinforce a cycle of poverty. Adult educators in these programs could help women examine the validity of socially constructed viewpoints and thereby help them to be more proactive.

Because informal and incidental learning are unstructured, it is easy to become trapped by blind spots about one's own needs, assumptions, and values that influence the way people frame a situation, and by misperceptions about one's own responsibility when errors occur. When people learn in families, groups, workplaces, or other social settings, their interpretation of a situation and consequent actions are highly influenced by social and cultural norms of others. Yet, people often do not deeply question their own or others' views. Power dynamics may distort the way in which they understand events. These issues make it imperative that we teach adult learners strategies to make this kind of learning both more visible and more rigorous.

Conclusion

We are pleased with the progress scholars have made in deepening our understanding of the nature of informal and incidental learning in the past ten years. It seems clear that these are the most pervasive forms of adult learning and that we can indeed enhance this kind of learning with educational intervention.

The studies noted in this chapter richly describe the processes and strategies learners use when learning informally and incidentally.

Yet there remain a number of interesting questions. First, without intervention or critical reflection, it is equally possible to hold incorrect as well as correct assumptions. More studies such as that currently being conducted by Wilson (2000) of hotel managers' defensive reasoning may help us learn more about the tacit processes by which individuals embed error. In fact, we suggest that with an incorrect frame on a problem, every step in the cycle is compromised so that we are solving the wrong problem and drawing incorrect inferences from the results we obtain.

We need to learn more about the interface between learning at the individual, team, and organizational levels. We have defined learning at the individual level as the way in which people make meaning and acquire knowledge and skill; learning at the team level as the mutual construction of new knowledge including the capacity for concerted, collaborative action; and learning at the organizational level as that which is embedded in systems, policies, procedures, work processes and information systems, organizational mental models, schema, and knowledge embedded in products and services. What are the nuances, the differences between and among these levels? To what extent are they accurate? What happens at the intersection of individual and team, of team and organization?

Finally, technology is changing the face of organizations and having an impact on the nature of informal and incidental learning. In fact, given the distributed, asynchronous nature of technology-facilitated interactions, more may be learned incidentally by learners reading between the lines. As we work to bring adult education to the Web, studies exploring how people learn in these settings are needed.

Informal and incidental learning can be enhanced with facilitation or increased awareness by the learner. Formal adult learning may also be enhanced if adult educators heed the lessons learned informally and incidentally. While much is known about these pervasive forms of adult learning, much remains to be learned.

References

Argyris, C., and Schön, D. *Theory in Practice: Increasing Professional Effectiveness.* San Francisco: Jossey-Bass, 1974.

Argyris, C., and Schön, D. *Organizational Learning: A Theory of Action Perspective.* San Francisco: Jossey-Bass, 1978.

Bandura, A. *Social Foundations of Thought and Action: A Social Cognitive Theory.* Englewood Cliffs, N.J.: Prentice-Hall, 1986.

Boud, D., Cohen, R., and Walker, D. (eds.) *Using Experience for Learning.* Buckingham, England: The Society for Research into Higher Education and Open University Press, 1993.

Callahan, M.H.W. *Case Study of an Advanced Technology Business Incubator as a Learning Environment.* Unpublished doctoral dissertation, The University of Georgia, Athens, 1999.

Candy, P. C. *Self Direction for Lifelong Learning: A Comprehensive Guide to Theory and Practice.* San Francisco: Jossey-Bass, 1991.

Carter, G. *Stroke Survivors: Finding Their Way Through Informal and Incidental Learning.* Unpublished doctoral dissertation, University of Texas, Austin, 1995.

Coombs, P., and Ahmed, M. *Attacking Rural Poverty: How Nonformal Education Can Help.* Baltimore: Johns Hopkins University Press, 1974.

Cseh, M. *Managerial Learning in the Transition to a Free Market Economy in Romanian Private Companies.* Unpublished doctoral dissertation, The University of Georgia, Athens, 1998.

Cseh, M., Watkins, K. E., and Marsick, V. J. "Re-conceptualizing Marsick and Watkins' Model of Informal and Incidental Learning in the Workplace." In K. P. Kuchinke (ed.), *Proceedings, Academy of Human Resource Development Conference, Volume I* (pp. 349–356), Baton Rouge, LA: Academy of Human Resource Development, 1999.

Dewey, J. *Experience and Education.* New York: Collier Books, 1938.

Garrick, J. *Informal Learning in the Workplace: Unmasking Human Resource Development.* London: Routledge, 1998.

Honey, P., and Mumford, A. *Capitalizing on Your Learning Style.* (2nd ed.) King of Prussia, PA: Organization Design and Development, 1989.

Jarvis, P. *Adult Learning in the Social Context.* London: Croom-Helm, 1987.

Knowles, M. *Informal Adult Education.* New York: Association Press, 1950.

Kolb, D. A. *Experiential Learning.* Englewood Cliffs, NJ: Prentice-Hall, 1984.

Lave, J., and Wenger, E. *Situated Learning—Legitimate Peripheral Participation.* Cambridge: Cambridge University Press, 1991.

Marsick, V. J., and Volpe, M. "The Nature of and Need for Informal Learning." In V. J. Marsick and M. Volpe (eds.), *Informal Learning on the Job,* Advances in Developing Human Resources, No. 3. San Francisco: Berrett Koehler, 1999.

Marsick, V. J., and Watkins, K. *Informal and Incidental Learning in the Workplace.* London and New York: Routledge, 1990.

Marsick, V. J., and Watkins, K. *Facilitating Learning Organizations: Making Learning Count.* Aldershot, England: Gower Publishers, 1999.

Menard, S.A.W. *Critical Learning Incidents of Female Army Nurse Vietnam Veterans and Their Perceptions of Organizational Culture in a Combat Area.* Unpublished doctoral dissertation, Abstracts International 55–01A (4651) (University Microfilm No. AAI9413556), University of Texas, Austin, 1993.

Mezirow, J. D. *Transformative Dimensions of Adult Learning.* San Francisco: Jossey-Bass, 1991.

Mocker, D. W., and Spear, G. E. *Lifelong Learning: Formal, Non-Formal, Informal and Self-Directed.* Columbus, OH: ERIC Clearinghouse on Adult, Career and Vocational Education, 1982.

Nonaka, I., and Takeuchi, H. *The Knowledge Creating Company.* New York: Oxford, 1995.

Polanyi, M. *The Tacit Dimension.* New York: Doubleday, 1967.

Reischmann, J. "Learning 'En Passant': The Forgotten Dimension." Paper presented at the American Association of Adult and Continuing Education Conference, 1986.

Revans, R. W. *The Origins and Growth of Action Learning.* Bickly, Kent: Chartwell-Bratt, and Lund, Sweden: Studenlitteratur, 1982.

Schön, D. A. *The Reflective Practitioner.* New York: Basic Books, 1983.

Scribner, S. "Thinking in Action: Some Characteristics of Practical Thought." In R. J. Sternberg and R. K. Wagner (eds.), *Practical Intelligence: Nature and Origins of Competence in the Everyday World.* Cambridge, England: Cambridge University Press, 1986.

Watkins, K. E., and Cervero, R. "Organizations as Contexts for Learning: Differentiating Opportunities and Experiences of a Certified Public Accountant." *Journal of Workplace Learning,* 2000, *12*(5), 187–194.

Watkins, K., and Marsick, V. J. *Sculpting the Learning Organization.* San Francisco: Jossey-Bass, 1993.

Watkins, K., and Marsick, V. J. *In Action: Creating the Learning Organization.* Arlington: ASTD Press, 1996.

Wenger, E. *Communities of Practice.* Cambridge: Cambridge University Press, 1998.

Wilson, J. *Defensive Reasoning of Hotel Managers.* Unpublished doctoral dissertation, The University of Georgia, Athens, 2000.

VICTORIA J. MARSICK is professor of adult education at Teacher's College, Columbia University. She is also the director of the Huber Institute for Transformative Learning at Columbia.

KAREN E. WATKINS is professor of adult education and interim director of the School of Leadership and Lifelong Learning at The University of Georgia.

4

How can we rethink some popular stereotypes about women's learning?

A New Look at Women's Learning

Elisabeth R. Hayes

Why *Women's* Learning?

Women's potentially distinctive characteristics as learners have been a topic of interest to scholars, educators, and women themselves for centuries. Noted Western (male) philosophers, ranging from Plato to Rousseau, questioned whether women could learn at all, or could at least engage in the kind of rational thought typically associated with "higher" learning. Women were described as the gender of "fruitful wombs and barren brains" (Hales, 1999, p. 240). Even within the last century, women's ability to learn has been questioned, or at least subordinated to their reproductive and affective capacities. A popular obstetrics textbook in the early twentieth century stated that "A woman has a head too small for intellect but just big enough for love" (Hales, 1999, p. 4). Such views prompted Charlotte Perkins Gilman, a prominent feminist in the late 1800s, to argue "the brain is not an organ of sex" (Hales, 1999, p. 241).

Our ideas about women as learners have come a long way, reinforced by women's success in formal education. While at one time women were excluded from higher education, they now constitute more than half of all bachelor's degree recipients. Girls and women tend to earn higher grades than boys and men (Howe and Strauss, 2000). "Women's ways of knowing" (Belenky, Clinchy, Goldberger, and Tarule, 1986), popularly characterized as collaborative and empathetic, have been promoted as more effective and appropriate ways of learning in the workplace and in formal education than the competitive, individualistic modes of knowing traditionally associated with men. Increasingly we have come to acknowledge the previously invisible yet significant informal learning that takes place in the traditionally female activities of motherhood and household management.

New Directions for Adult and Continuing Education, no. 89, Spring 2001 © Jossey-Bass, A Publishing Unit of John Wiley & Sons, Inc.

However, the nature of women's learning remains controversial. Several years ago, I and a colleague, Daniele Flannery, reviewed a large body of literature on women, learning, and education, hoping to develop a comprehensive picture of women's learning. In some literature, we found a litany of characteristics reminiscent of *Men Are from Mars, Women Are from Venus* (Gray, 1992). Women and men learners have been described as speaking "different languages." Women are oriented toward sharing feelings and communicating empathy, while men share information and give advice; women are thought to prefer solving problems in groups, while men prefer independent problem solving. The descriptions have some disturbing similarities to centuries-old stereotypes of women, stereotypes that were used to question women's learning capacities.

Indeed, some scholars argue against a search for distinctive attributes of women's learning, claiming that any actual differences are inconsequential and that women's "difference" will be used to assert women's "deficiency" as learners. Indeed, we found little convincing evidence to support most assertions about women as learners or educational practices for women based on these beliefs (Flannery and Hayes, 2000). Women's learning has received growing attention from researchers in the last two decades, but conclusions drawn from this research remain questionable. Overgeneralization about differences between women and men is a very common pitfall. For example, sex differences in mathematics ability have been exaggerated and distorted in scholarship and the popular media (Crawford, 1995; Hyde, 1990). While there is actually more overlap than difference in male and female test scores, and factors other than sex, such as age and race, have a significant impact, the "superior" mathematics ability of males has been widely acclaimed and even attributed to genetics or hormones. Such conclusions contribute to a "generic" category of women that renders invisible the considerable diversity among women as learners. Generalizations about groups of women based on attributes such as race and ethnicity are derived from the experiences of only a handful of women, with little attention to differences within such groups.

In this chapter, I will encourage readers to take a "new look" at some popular beliefs about women as learners. I will draw on some recent conceptualizations of gender and learning to suggest alternative perspectives that might serve as a basis for understanding and supporting women's learning in a variety of settings. My purpose is not to encourage an emphasis on difference, but rather an appreciation of gender as a crucial aspect of our lives and learning.

Popular Beliefs About Women as Learners

Two prevalent, interrelated sets of beliefs about women as learners relate to the significance of relationships, or "connection," in women's learning and women's presumed preferences for subjective and affective ways of learning.

Relationship. The significance of relationship in women's lives has been widely touted ever since Carol Gilligan (1982), along with other psychologists such as Jean Baker Miller (1986), popularized the idea that a woman defines herself—and views her world—primarily in relationship to others. Numerous other scholars have supported the idea that women's psychological development is oriented more toward increasing intimacy with others than toward autonomy (the orientation typically associated with men's psychological development). Various explanations for this relational orientation have been proposed, such as the idea that mothers encourage their daughters to identify and affiliate with them as women, while they encourage their sons to differentiate and strive for separation as men (Miller, 1986). This centrality of relationship has led to recommendations that educational programs for women should emphasize collaboration, support, and affiliation, as well as to critiques of gender bias in the emphasis on autonomy and self-direction in much adult education literature and practice (Flannery, 1994).

Another perspective on relationship in women's learning concerns women's ways of acquiring new knowledge. The concept of "connected knowing" was introduced by the authors of *Women's Ways of Knowing* (Belenky, Clinchy, Goldberger, and Tarule, 1986), which became perhaps the most influential publication about women's learning in the last two decades. Connected knowing was described as embracing new ideas and seeking to understand different points of view. Connected knowing was contrasted with "separate knowing," characterized by taking a more adversarial stance toward new ideas and looking for flaws in logic and reasoning. While the authors identified a variety of ways of knowing used by the women in their research, they asserted that connected learning was preferred by the largest number. They proposed "connected teaching" to support this way of knowing. Connected teaching was intended to contrast with traditional modes of education that emphasize separate knowing, and, presumably, conflict with women's preferred modes of learning. These ideas influenced the design of many educational programs for women, particularly in higher education (Stanton, 1996).

The idea that relationships figure prominently in the lives of many women is hardly surprising given women's traditional roles as caretakers in the home and their concentration in caretaking roles in the workplace, such as teaching and nursing. These theories offer intriguing ideas about how relationships might influence women's learning—ideas that have great appeal because of how they resonate with the experience of many women. Unfortunately, this orientation toward relationship is frequently interpreted in simplistic terms, leading to beliefs such as that women learn best in groups rather than alone. Furthermore, emphasizing an orientation toward relationship can fuel stereotypes that women are not, or cannot be, competitive, autonomous, or self-directed.

Subjectivity, Intuition, and Emotion. Women's presumed orientations toward human relationships are linked to characterizations of women as reliant on subjective, intuitive, and affective ways of learning (Flannery, 2000).

Establishing rapport with others, nurturing them, and responding to their needs depend on appreciation for the subjective, sensitivity to affect as well as intellect, and understanding that goes beyond the purely rational.

These beliefs about women's learning are not particularly new. The precursors of modern beliefs can be traced back to Greek philosophers and the Western Enlightenment philosophical tradition of creating a dualism of mind and body, emotion and intellect. Women were associated with the bodily, emotional, nonrational side of the dichotomy, and thus considered to be incapable of reason. This belief was used as a rationale for excluding women from political participation, higher education, and the workplace outside the home. More recently, feminists as well as other scholars have asserted the value and importance of nonrational modes of thought, while pointing out the limitations of an overreliance on rationality. While this revaluing of the nonrational promises to benefit everyone, men as well as women, the extent to which women really are more inclined toward affective or subjective modes of thought remains questionable. Similar to a focus on relationship, associating women primarily with intuition or affect can reinforce the idea that women are not well-suited for logical, objective, rational thought.

How Gender Affects Learning

How can we come to a better, more inclusive understanding of women as learners? As a starting point, we must revisit our beliefs about gender and the role it plays in our learning. The most common theories about women's learning have approached gender from a psychological perspective, emphasizing the impact of women's socialization into gender specific roles or their relationships with parents and other caregivers. The changing nature of gender roles, however, renders generalizations based on these theories somewhat suspect. Recent studies of brain functioning have led to renewed interest in biological explanations for differences in women's and men's learning processes, prompting some authors to proclaim the existence of a "female brain" (Hales, 1999, p. 240), in contrast to Gilman's separation of sex and the brain a century ago. The results of this research, such as the finding that more parts of women's brains are active in certain cognitive tasks than in men's brains, have led some authors to claim that women's brains are "a model of connectedness" (Hales, 1999, p. 12). However, the significance of these differences in terms of actual learning abilities or performance has yet to be established.

This emphasis on psychological and biological theories about women's learning is perhaps not surprising, given the long-standing view of learning as primarily cognitive. More recently, learning theorists have begun to explore the social dimensions of learning, arguing that all learning is inextricably intertwined with the context in which it occurs. Gendered behaviors and characteristics, or our conceptions of masculinity and femininity, also have been increasingly theorized as products of socially and culturally determined belief systems, rather than rooted in purely psychological or biological sex differences (Crawford, 1995). These belief systems create different expectations and norms for people of each sex. We experience considerable social pressure to conform to gendered norms, though we each choose to conform or not in different ways. For example, if a social norm dictates that "self-assertiveness" is inappropriate for women, one female student might choose to be quiet or self-deprecating in order to maintain her "feminine" identity, though these behaviors might raise questions about her academic ability. Another woman might choose to be more assertive, risking negative judgments about her femininity in favor of expressing her knowledge and confidence. In each case, gender affects both behavior and its outcomes.

This view of gender suggests that attributes of women's learning are not innate, fixed, and uniform across situations ("essential" attributes of women), but are integrally connected to a particular set of situational, social, and historical circumstances, and thus changeable as those circumstances change. However, at any point in time these gendered belief systems can contribute to different patterns in women's and men's knowledge and approaches to learning. Sandra Harding (1996) describes the existence of "gender cultures" within broader cultures of society, such as the "masculine" cultures of the military or sports and the "feminine" cultures of the fashion world or elementary schools. While women and men can be found in both cultures, these cultures shape their experiences in different ways, giving them the opportunity to acquire different sorts of knowledge and abilities. As stereotypical examples, Harding notes that women may have more opportunities to interact with babies, while men have more opportunities to interact with car motors.

Furthermore, Harding states, the system of gender relations can give women and men different interests and concerns even when they are in similar situations. Accordingly, knowledge acquired from the same situations may be different. To use another stereotypical example, a woman with primary responsibility for childrearing, when seeking a job may gather detailed information about potential employers' policies toward maternity leave and provision of childcare. In contrast, a man with primary responsibility for supporting a wife and family may seek to gain more knowledge of employers' health care plans and life insurance policies.

Gender relations also may lead women and men to develop different ways of learning. Some theorists suggest that since women have traditionally been in positions of less power than men, as a means of survival they have become more attuned to identifying and understanding the feelings and perspectives of others, leading perhaps to the orientation toward "connected" learning popularly ascribed to women. As with gender relations, these gendered ways of knowing may differ by society, culture, ethnic group, locality, and so on, thus potentially resulting in differing learning preferences among women as well as between women and men. For example, several of my African American women colleagues feel that conflict and strong emotions are essential for a meaningful learning experience. Their beliefs seem to reflect a cultural upbringing in which such conflict reflected an authentic engagement with the topic and with other people. In contrast, many of my white female colleagues (including myself) are very uncomfortable with such strong emotions in the classroom, undoubtedly a link to a different cultural proscription against overt conflict.

Gender and Educational Practice

How can this understanding of gender as a type of social relation, which is experienced and acted upon in different ways by different people, inform our practice as adult educators? Certainly it offers nothing quite as simple and concrete as the popular beliefs I described earlier, such as "women prefer connected learning." In fact, this perspective requires us to question any such generalizations and assumptions about women's learning—and men's. It can be tempting to simply ignore gender, perhaps in the name of treating each person as a unique individual. Ignoring gender can make us blind to the significant impact that it can have on our learners, and to ways that we can improve learning experiences for all learners.

As Jane Hugo (2000) has pointed out, how adult educators use any kind of information about women's learning will depend on their commitment to different educational goals and purposes. Educators who primarily seek to help learners acquire knowledge of content may draw different implications than, for example, educators who emphasize the personal development of learners, or who wish to promote social change. Here I will describe just a few examples related to different educational goals.

If we focus on content learning, we can use Harding's conception of gendered knowledge systems to consider how gender might affect the prior knowledge that learners bring to bear on the subject matter of an educational activity, what kind of knowledge they might consider to be important, and how they interpret new information. We can be alert to potential gender patterns while trying to avoid gender stereotypes. The value of identifying learners' current knowledge and interests as a basis for instruction is an adult education truism. By using gender (in combination with other influential factors such as race and class) as a lens for understanding *why* learners may have some kinds of knowledge and not others, why they have some interests and not others, we can gain more insight into appropriate instructional approaches and ways of presenting subject matter. Let's use a basic math class as an example. An educator might seek more information about how her learners use mathematical skills outside of the classroom, and how these skills are linked to gender roles. She might discover that the women have developed sophisticated strategies for estimating discounts or for comparison shopping. She might also find that they use certain tools in their mathematical reasoning, such as drawing pictures or using homemade measuring tools. The educator can use this information in a variety of ways, from creating relevant examples to incorporating learners' own math strategies into classroom activities as a means of facilitating content learning.

With an orientation toward personal development, educators can engage learners in identifying the gender belief systems that have affected them as learners, and in challenging those beliefs that might limit their learning. Returning to the math class example, the educator might encourage learners to explore the gendered nature of mathematics and how gender has affected their personal identities as mathematics learners. They might reflect on their experiences in school as children and teenagers, asking questions such as "How were the experiences of girls and boys with math similar and different?" "What did these experiences teach you about girls and boys as learners of mathematics?" "How do those experiences influence you now?" Similar questions can be raised about their experiences with math in the home or in workplaces. Sharing these reflections in groups enables learners to identify patterns of broader belief systems, to consider how those belief systems affected them in similar and different ways, and to consider how they might resist those beliefs that interfere with learning.

If educators seek to promote social change, they might explore with learners how gendered beliefs are acted upon, recreated, and transformed in the classroom. They might examine the potentially gendered nature of the knowledge that is presented in mathematics textbooks, and how gender affects their responses to these texts. They might explore their stereotypes about women and men as mathematics learners, and how these stereotypes are reinforced or challenged in their own experiences. They might learn to use math through activities that enable them to question current beliefs about gender and math; for example, by examining the statistics used to support women's inferior math abilities or by collecting and analyzing their own data on gender and participation in higher level math courses.

Taking a new look at women's learning can reveal more complexity and dynamism than we initially might have discerned. It offers us greater challenges, but also greater opportunities to create learning experiences that are supportive of both women and men.

References

Belenky, M. F., Clinchy, B. M., Goldberger, N .R., and Tarule, J. M. *Women's Ways of Knowing: The Development of Self, Voice, and Mind.* New York: Basic Books, 1986.

Crawford, M. *Talking Difference: On Gender and Language.* Thousand Oaks, CA: Sage, 1995.

Flannery, D. D. "Changing Dominant Understandings of Adults as Learners." In E. Hayes and S.A.J. Colin (eds.), *Confronting Racism and Sexism.* New Directions for Adult and Continuing Education, no. 61. San Francisco: Jossey-Bass, 1994.

Flannery, D. D. "Connection." In E. Hayes, D. D. Flannery, and others, *Women as Learners: The Significance of Gender in Adult Learning.* San Francisco: Jossey-Bass, 2000.

Flannery, D. D., and Hayes, E. "Women's Learning: A Kaleidoscope." In E. Hayes, D. D. Flannery, and others, *Women as Learners: The Significance of Gender in Adult Learning.* San Francisco: Jossey-Bass, 2000.

Gilligan, C. *In a Different Voice: Psychological Theory and Women's Development.* Cambridge, Mass.: Harvard University Press, 1982.

Gray, J. *Men Are from Mars, Women Are from Venus.* New York: HarperCollins, 1992.

Hales, D. *Just Like a Woman: How Gender Science Is Redefining What Makes Us Female.* New York: Bantam Books, 1999.

Harding, S. "Gendered Ways of Knowing and the Epistemological Crisis of the West." In N. R. Goldberger, J. M. Tarule, B. M. Clinchy, and M. F. Belenky (eds.), *Knowledge, Difference, and Power: Essays Inspired by Women's Ways of Knowing.* New York: Basic Books, 1996.

Howe, N., and Strauss, W. *Millenials Rising: The Next Generation.* New York: Random House, 2000.

Hugo, J. "Perspectives on Practice" In E. Hayes, D. D. Flannery, and others, *Women as Learners: The Significance of Gender in Adult Learning.* San Francisco: Jossey-Bass, 2000.

Hyde, J. "Gender Comparisons of Mathematics Attitudes and Affect: A Meta-analysis." *Psychology of Women Quarterly,* 1990, *14*(3), 299–324.

Miller, J. B. *Toward a New Psychology of Women.* Boston: Beacon Press, 1986.

Stanton, A. "Reconfiguring Teaching and Knowing." In N. R. Goldberger, J. M. Tarule, B. M. Clinchy, and M. F. Belenky (eds.), *Knowledge, Difference, and Power: Essays Inspired by Women's Ways of Knowing.* New York: Basic Books, 1996.

ELISABETH R. HAYES *is professor of curriculum and instruction and a faculty member in the Graduate Program in Continuing and Vocational Education at the University of Wisconsin-Madison. She is coauthor of* Women as Learners *(Jossey-Bass, 2000).*

5

Adult learning takes place in context where tools and the context intersect with interaction among people.

Context-Based Adult Learning

Catherine A. Hansman

A few years ago, with a newly acquired master's degree in secondary education, I was hired by a midwestern university to teach writing to traditional and adult students in a university developmental writing program. My educational background as a musician and my work experience as a computer programmer had not prepared me to teach writing to adults. Colleagues hired with me also had diverse backgrounds; no one had ever taught writing in a university setting before. The problem became very apparent to all of us: How could we, in the week between when we were hired and when we were to start teaching, learn to be teachers of writing?

The university's solution to this problem was a required week-long series of English Department–sponsored workshops that incorporated lecture-style classes to indoctrinate us with the guidelines and rules that the English Department wished us to use to teach and grade papers. We heard talks from more accomplished writing teachers concerning their experiences, examined sample assignments and student written essays, and listened to recommendations from others about how to teach. In short, in a state of passive attentiveness and decreasing interest and awareness, we heard theories and abstract concepts about teaching writing. The obvious assumption by the planners of this workshop was that we would carry away knowledge about teaching writing from these workshops and apply it to our own classrooms. By the end of the week, we were, in the university's eyes, teachers of writing and ready to face a classroom of adult and traditional-aged university students.

But how did we really learn to be teachers? Our actual learning about teaching writing happened over time and was mediated by the experiences we had both in and out of writing classrooms. It was shaped by our interacting with students, discussing assignments and students with other instructors, observing each other's classes, trying new assignments and ways of teaching, reflecting on our practice, and negotiating among the English department's and the university's rules and regulations. Along with our experiences in the classroom, the tools we used to teach (texts, computers, assignments) and the interactions with students, other writing teachers, and the administrators of the writing program at the university shaped our learning. Our authentic learning about teaching writing consisted of more than lectures about assignments and grading papers; it was in the unplanned intersection of people, culture, tools, and context.

My real-world experience of learning to teach writing is crucial to ideas of context-based adult learning. Indeed, adult education as a field has always valued learning from experience and collaboration. Dewey (1916) contends that "[t]he social environment . . . is truly educative in the effects in the degree in which an individual shares or participates in some conjoint activity. By doing his (sic) share in the associated activity, the individual appropriates the purpose which actuates it, becomes familiar with its methods and subject matters, acquires needed skills, and is saturated with its emotional spirit" (p. 26). In a similar fashion, Lindemann (1926) declares that "the approach to adult education will be via the route of situations, not subjects" (p. 6).

The ideas of the social context as central to learning have gained importance in discussions of learning in adulthood. Wilson (1993) argues that "learning is an everyday event that is social in nature because it occurs with other people; it is 'tool dependent' because the setting provides mechanisms (computers, maps, measuring cups) that aid, and more important, structure the cognitive process; and finally, it is the interaction with the setting itself in relation to its social and tool dependent nature that determines the learning" (p. 73). In other words, learning in context is paying attention to the interaction and intersection among people, tools, and context within a learning situation. More important, for adult educators who plan and teach, it is understanding how to plan and design programs for adult learners that will profoundly shape learning. And finally, it is incorporating the learners' developmental needs, ideas, and cultural context into the learning experience. This chapter will examine theories of learning in context in adulthood and discuss how these ideas can be used in adult learning situations.

Learning Outside the Mind

From a historic viewpoint, behaviorist educational practices and psychological conceptions of learning have mirrored demands from business and industry to produce productive workers (Bonk and Kim, 1998). Behaviorism, punish-and-reward systems, and quantifiable methods of evaluation all contributed to a "factory model of learning" (Toffler, 1990). From this perspective, "knowledge is unchanging and transitive" (Brown and Duguid, 1996, p. 49), and once learned, is then easily transported from the particular learning situation to different contexts in which the knowledge can be put to work (Brown, Collins, and Duguid, 1989). Learning, then, is seen as something that happens inside the brain, separated from the experience and the context of the learning situation.

But as Merriam and Caffarella (1999) contend, "Adult learning does not occur in a vacuum" (p. 22). In contrast to psychological and behavioral understandings of learning, sociocultural models posit that learning is not something that happens, or is just inside the head, but instead is shaped by the context, culture, and tools in the learning situation. One of the earliest pioneers of sociocultural learning theory was twentieth-century Russian psychologist L. S. Vygotsky, who based his work on the concept that all human activities take place in a cultural context with many levels of interactions, shared beliefs, values, knowledge, skills, structured relationships, and symbol systems (Wertsch, del Rio, and Alvarez, 1995). These interactions and activities are mediated through the use of tools, either technical (machines, computers, calculators) or psychological (language, counting, writing, and strategies for learning), provided by the culture (Vygotsky, 1978, 1999). These tools ensure that linguistically created meanings have shared social meanings.

Vygotsky's theories advanced an understanding and enhancement of how children learn and were essential to the development of other theories of learning in context. They provided a way to understand technical and psychological tools and how to use these them in practice. Many of his ideas have been incorporated into situated cognition as another theory of context-based learning.

Situating Learning: Understanding Situated Cognition

The core idea in situated cognition is that learning is inherently social in nature. The nature of the interactions among learners, the tools they use within these interactions, the activity itself, and the social context in which the activity takes place shape learning. In her ethnographic study of how adults used math in real-world contexts such as grocery stores, Lave (1988) concluded that learning is a reoccurring process in which adults act and interact within their social situations. In her study, adults who were taught a "school" version of how to calculate mathematical problems were observed and interviewed concerning how they used the same type of mathematical equations in the real world of grocery store shopping. She found that the grocery items, coupons, and "in-store specials" themselves became tools for solving mathematical problems, while the grocery store and the social interactions with other shoppers or store workers were the social context for learning. Lave (1996) argues that it is not enough to "add situated contexts to learning experiences . . . a more promising alternative lies in treating relations among people, tools, activity as they are given in social practice" (p. 7). In other words, real-world contexts, where there are social relationships and tools, make the best learning environments.

How is situated cognition similar yet different from other forms of experiential learning? Experiential learning emphasizes doing the task in order to learn it, and this "doing" may include self-directed learning activities. The learner may receive prior instruction before performing the task, then do the task on his or her own. For instance, since moving into my seventy-year-old house, I have had to repair (or at least attempt to repair) numerous problems with plumbing. In order to make these repairs, I read books and "old home" magazines, watched home-repair shows, and, when all else failed, asked my brothers (who live in different cities) for advice. But my real learning about plumbing happens from the actual experience of working on the plumbing—handling the unfamiliar wrenches, crawling around the pipes, and trying to figure out which part goes where without causing more damage. This is real experiential learning—the learning is in the doing or the experience.

But how would this experience look if I were able to learn plumbing and old-home repairs from a situated framework? I might still take all the initial steps of reading and schooling myself on plumbing, and I would definitely still "do" something. However, since situated cognition emphasizes interaction between the learner and other learners and tools in a sociocultural context, I might also join a home-repair club or group of old-home owners interested in working on their houses. We might meet at each other's homes to work together and problem solve a particular plumbing problem. The more experienced members in the group may teach the less experienced. I might not only learn solutions to my immediate plumbing problems but also solutions to possible future problems sure to eventually occur in older houses. The context of older houses and the dialogue between and among old-home owners with plumbing problems may take place as the task is being performed and therefore is integrally woven within the learning experience.

From a situated view, people learn as they participate and become intimately involved with a community or culture of learning, interacting with the community and learning to understand and participate in its history, assumptions, and cultural values and rules (Lave and Wenger, 1991, Fenwick, 2000). Thus, "learning is situated in interactions among peripheral participants and full participants in a community of meaning. These interactions take place in the context of practice and are characterized by modeling of both mastery of practice and the process of gaining mastery" (Jacobson, 1996, p. 23). These ideas of learning from more experienced members of a community and participation in cultures of practice have led to a number of concepts of planning and managing learning situations that can incorporate situated views of learning. Two of these concepts, cognitive apprenticeships (Farmer, Buckmaster, and LeGrand Brandt, 1992; LeGrand Brandt, Farmer, and Buckmaster, 1993; Rogoff, 1990, 1993, 1995) and communities of practice (Lave and Wenger, 1991; Brown and Gray, 1995;

Wenger, 1998), offer adult educators basic concepts and tools to better situate learning.

Situating Cognition in the World of Practice

Cognitive Apprenticeships. Rogoff (1990, 1993, 1995) proposes that learning involves development in personal, interpersonal, and community processes. These phases are not necessarily sequential and are somewhat fluid, as members may move between phases. One mechanism for learning at these levels is through cognitive apprenticeships. LeGrand Brandt, Farmer, and Buckmaster (1993), for example, describe cognitive apprenticeship in continuing professional education as occurring in five sequential phases: modeling, approximating, fading, self-directed learning, and generalizing. *Modeling* occurs in two parts: behavioral modeling allows learners to observe performance of an activity by experienced members of a community, while cognitive modeling allows experienced members to share "tricks of the trade" with newer members. *Approximating* allows learners to try out the activity while articulating their thoughts about what they plan to do and why, and after the activity, reflecting about what they did and how it is different from the expert's performance. In this phase, to minimize risk while at the same time allowing learners to approximate the real experience, role models provide *scaffolding,* which takes the form of physical aids, modeling tasks, and coaching. In the *fading* process, scaffolding and other support gradually decrease as learners' abilities increase. *Self-directed* learning takes place as learners practice doing the real thing, adapting what is necessary from models and working on their own, receiving assistance only at their request. Finally, students *generalize* what they have learned through discussions and relate what they have learned to subsequent practice situations.

In the academic world of universities, cognitive apprenticeships can frame how newcomers to academe learn university life and expectations. For example, my job teaching developmental writing to adult students was about more than just teaching students the fundamentals of composition. It was also about helping students understand and become participants in academic culture. Instead of only listening to lectures and prescriptions about writing processes, students engaged in the activity of writing; scaffolding consisted of computers as tools for writing, writing labs, and discussions about writing situations and expectations. Students had dialogues among themselves, with more-experienced students, and with instructors about writing processes and general concerns about academic culture; thus, they moved through apprenticeships with coaching and scaffolding to some level of participatory appropriation within academic culture (Hansman, 1995; Hansman and Wilson, 1998). Graduate students also move through and among these phases as they work with their major professors as teaching assistants and as researchers, writing theses and dissertations. Indeed, new faculty, especially those who are mentored, learn academic life through apprenticeship.

Communities of Practice. Communities of practice are self-organized and selected groups of people who share a common sense of purpose and a desire to learn and know what each other knows (Lave and Wenger, 1991; Brown and Gray, 1995; Brown and Duguid, 1996; Wenger, 1998). These groups can be somewhat informal in nature, for example, as basic as mealtime discussions of problems inherent in shared practice. Some may only be connected through e-mail or other on-line means. They are self-organized by the members themselves and may exist within larger organizational structures. Wenger (1998) describes the dimensions of the relationships within communities of practice as several concepts: *mutual engagement* of the participants that allows them to do what they need to do and binds members into a social entity; *joint enterprise* resulting from a "collective process of negotiations that reflects the full complexity of mutual engagement" (p. 77); and a *shared repertoire* of communal resources that belongs to the community of practice and includes "routines, words, tools, ways of doing things, stories, gestures, symbols, genres, actions, or concepts that the community has produced or adopted in the course of its existence, and which have become part of its practice" (p. 83).

To return to the example of learning to teach writing, I engaged in a self-organized community of practice of other novice and expert writing instructors. We shared a joint interest and were mutually engaged in understanding what makes up good teaching practice; at the same time we shared a repertoire of writing assignments and other classroom routines and tools to improve our practice. Similarly, Daley's (1999) study of how professionals learn focused on the ways novice and expert nurses understood their own learning processes, how they learned to learn, how they could teach themselves, and how they built their own bank of knowledge. Most important, however, was that the expert nurses described learning so they could share their knowledge with novice nurses while at the same time learning from the process of sharing.

"Passion, commitment, and identification with the group's expertise" (Wenger and Snyder, 2000b, p. 142) is the glue that holds these groups together. The group's life cycle is also determined by the value these qualities provide to group members, not by organizational values or institutional schedules. The power in communities of practice is that they organize themselves, set their own agendas, and establish their own leadership. Thus, members of communities of practice may feel more connected to these small communities than larger organizational cultures. However, Wenger and Snyder (2000a) claim that "in the new economy, learning architects are embracing the natural designs of group learning and translating those designs to new organizational cultures and approaches" (p. 2). For example, at Hill's Pet Nutrition facility, line technicians formed a group that met weekly to discuss successes and future challenges, and to gather expertise from each other. This group met in a company conference room, but otherwise was self-supporting. Through their meetings, members of the group were able to propose a new system of pneumatic tubes to replace balky conveyer belts (Wenger and Snyder, 2000a). Although management initially rejected this idea, expertise knowledge from the line technicians combined with evidence from groups at other plants eventually led to the change. The result was rewarding for the company (fewer line delays) and for the group (developing problem solving and abilities to run the plant effectively).

The ideas of *cognitive apprenticeships* and *communities of practice* can provide adult educators with tools to redesign workplace and school learning to allow these communities to form. Brown and Duguid (1996) describe the challenge organizations and schools face "to redesign the learning environment so that newcomers can legitimately and peripherally participate in authentic social practice in rich and productive ways, in short, make it possible for learners to 'steal' the knowledge they need" (p. 49).

The Promise of Context-Based Learning

Wilson's journal chapter, "The Promise of Situated Cognition" (1993), predicted a future for adult learning that would take into account activity, culture, and tools. Yet eight years later, the ideas of learning in context and situated cognition have yet to be fully explored and developed in adult education. In my view, it is imperative that adult educators understand that learning can take place in many settings and therefore design programs that incorporate tools, context, and social interactions with others. These programs could take the form of internships, apprenticeships, and formal and informal mentoring programs that provide adult learners with real-world, context-based learning. Planners could also support situations for adults to participate in communities of practice in the cafeterias, student lounges, or computer labs (Bonk and Kim, 1998). Membership in professional organizations can also provide adults with the cultural context, tools, and social learning to progress in their fields or professions. For leisure learning, adults may participate in travel clubs, where the travel itself to new cultures and contexts provides the intersection of culture, tools, and contexts that shape learning.

Theories of context-based learning provide a powerful and egalitarian way of viewing knowledge production. Knowledge, skills, and abilities of those whom Lave (1988) refers to as "just plain folks"—those who historically and traditionally have not been counted as "experts," such as the women in Lave's grocery study or the line technicians at Hill's Pet Nutrition Facility—are valued. Viewing knowledge and learning through this lens allows adult educators and program planners to create or enhance contexts for adult learning that allow learners to share in the design, process, and evaluation of their learning activities. As active members of communities of practice, adult learners can discover, shape, and make explicit their own knowledge, thus intensifying the intriguing discussion about what counts for knowledge and learning in adulthood. Last, the real promise of context-based learning is that "knowing" of "just plain folks" is valued, thus enhancing the knowledge and development of adult learning theory.

References

Bonk, J. B., and Kim, K. A. "Extending Sociocultural Theory to Adult Learning." In M. C. Smith and T. Pourchot (eds.), *Adult Learning and Development: Perspectives from Educational Psychology*. Mahwah, NJ: Lawrence Erlbaum Associates, 1998.

Brown, J., and Duguid, P. "Stolen Knowledge." In H. McLellen (ed.), *Situated Learning Perspectives*. Englewood Cliffs, NJ: Educational Technology Publications, 1996.

Brown, J. and Gray, S. "The People Are the Company." *FastCompany*, November 1995, 78.

Brown, J. S., Collins, A., and Duguid, P. "Situated Cognition and the Culture of Learning." *Educational Researcher*, 1989, *18*(1), 32–42.

Daley, B. J. "Novice to Expert: An Exploration of How Professionals Learn." *Adult Education Quarterly*, 1999, *49*(4), 133–42.

Dewey, J. *Democracy and Education: An Introduction into the Philosophy of Education*. New York: McMillan, 1916.

Farmer, J. A., Buckmaster, A., and LeGrand Brandt, B. "Cognitive Apprenticeship: Implications for Continuing Professional Education." In H. K. Morris Baskett and V. Marsick (eds.), *Professionals' Ways of Knowing: Findings on How to Improve Professional Education*. New Directions for Adult and Continuing Education, no. 55, San Francisco: Jossey-Bass, 1992.

Fenwick, T. "Expanding Conceptions of Experiential Learning: A Review of the Five Contemporary Perspectives on Cognition." *Adult Education Quarterly*, 2000, *50*(4), 248–272.

Hansman, C. A. *Writing with Computers: A Study of Adult Developmental Writers*. Unpublished doctoral dissertation, Department of Adult and Community Education, Ball State University, 1995.

Hansman, C. A., and Wilson, A. L. "Teaching Writing in Community Colleges: A Situated View of How Adults Learn to Write in Computer-Based Writing Classrooms." *Community College Review*, 1998, *26*(1), 27–41.

Jacobson, W. "Learning, Culture, and Learning Culture." *Adult Education Quarterly*, 1996, *47*(1), 15–28.

Lave, J. *Cognition in Practice: Mind, Mathematics, and Culture in Everyday Life*. Cambridge, England: Cambridge University Press, 1988.

Lave, J. "The Practice of Learning." In S. Chaiklin and J. Lave (eds.), *Understanding Practice: Perspectives on Activity and Context*. Cambridge, England: Cambridge University Press, 1996.

Lave, J., and Wenger, E. *Situated Learning: Legitimate Peripheral Participation. New York: Cambridge University Press, 1991*.

LeGrand Brandt, B., Farmer, J. A., and Buckmaster, A. "Cognitive Apprenticeship Approach to Helping Adults Learn." In D. D. Flannery (ed.), *Applying Cognitive Learning Theory to Adult Learning*. New Directions for Adult and Continuing Education, no.59, San Francisco: Jossey-Bass, 1993.

Lindemann, E. *The Meaning of Adult Education*. New York: New Republic, 1926.

Merriam, S., and Caffarella, R. *Learning in Adulthood* (2nd Ed.). San Francisco: Jossey-Bass, 1999.

Rogoff, B. *Apprenticeship in Thinking: Cognitive Development in Social Context*. New York: Oxford University Press, 1990.

Rogoff, B. "Children's Guided Participation and Participatory Appropriation in Sociocultural Activity." In R. Wozniak and K. Fischer (eds.), *Development in Context: Acting and Thinking in Specific Environments.* Hillsdale, NJ: Erlbaum, 1993.

Rogoff, B. "Observing Sociocultural Activity in Three Planes: Participatory Appropriation, Guided Participation, and Apprenticeship." In J. Wertsch, P. del Rio, and A. Alvarez (eds.), *Sociocultural Studies of the Mind.* Cambridge, England: Cambridge University Press, 1995.

Toffler, A. *Powershift: Knowledge, Wealth, and Violence at the Edge of the 21st Century.* New York: Bantam Books, 1990.

Vygotsky, L. S. *Mind in Society: The Development of Higher Psychological Processes.* Cambridge, MA: Harvard University Press, 1978.

Vygotsky, L. S. *Thought and Language.* Cambridge, MA: The MIT Press, 1999.

Wenger, E. *Communities of Practice.* Cambridge, England: Cambridge University Press, 1998.

Wenger, E., and Snyder, W. "Learning in Communities." *LINEzine,* Summer 2000a, online at http://www.linezine.com/1/features/ewwsclc.

Wenger, E., and Snyder, W. "Communities of Practice: The Organizational Frontier." *Harvard Business Review,* Jan.-Feb., 2000b, 139–145.

Wertsch, J., del Rio, P, and Alvarez, A. "History, Action and Mediation." In J. Wertsch, P. del Rio, and A. Alvarez (eds.), *Sociocultural Studies of the Mind.* Cambridge, England: Cambridge University Press, 1995.

Wilson, A. L. "The Promise of Situated Cognition." In S. Merriam (ed.), *An Update on Adult Learning Theory.* New Directions for Adult and Continuing Education, no.57, San Francisco: Jossey-Bass, 1993.

CATHERINE A. HANSMAN is assistant professor and program director of graduate studies in Adult Learning and Development at Cleveland State University, Cleveland, Ohio.

6

This chapter characterizes and compares knowledge, power, and learning in the critical and postmodern theoretical worldviews.

Critical and Postmodern Perspectives on Adult Learning

Deborah W. Kilgore

Wouldn't it be nice if there were a generic learner who acquired knowledge in one or a few predictable ways? Wouldn't it be even better if we all agreed what knowledge was worth acquiring? Our models of learning would be brilliant guides to successful outcomes, and educators couldn't go wrong if they simply followed the bouncing ball of cause to effect, stimulus to response.

However, with the increasing inclusion of diverse participants in the conversation about adult education, it has become clear that there is no such thing as one kind of learner, one learning goal, one way to learn, nor one setting in which learning takes place. Many theorists have convincingly demonstrated that commonly held assumptions about generic learners and learning are irrelevant and even willfully oppressive when recklessly applied to all kinds of people without regard for their unique life experiences and attributes such as race, class, and gender. Furthermore, theorists have contributed new ways of understanding who learns and how, where, and why.

The theoretical perspectives of those who challenge neat and thus exclusionary models of adult learning often fall within the broad categories of critical and postmodern theory. Critical and postmodern theorists alike believe that knowledge is socially constructed and takes form in the eyes of the knower, rather than being acquired from an existing reality that resides "out there." Theorists from both perspectives are also interested in power as a factor in determining what and how we come to know a lot about certain things and not others, and have certain ideas while not others. Different individuals and groups see the world from different positions, some having more power than others. From either a critical or a postmodern perspective, learning is a process of receiving and creating communicative messages or "discourses" about the social world.

Although there is some overlap between the two paradigms, I will attempt in this chapter to compare and contrast the ways knowledge and power are conceptualized in each. From this categorization of worldviews will stem a distinction between how critical and postmodern theorists view adult learning. By classifying and assessing these two perspectives, I proceed in typically "modern" fashion, a manner the postmodern world rejects (Rosenau, 1992).

Knowledge and Learning

From either a critical or a postmodern perspective, knowledge is socially constructed and situated in a particular context. The primary difference between the two worldviews is that critical theorists assume that rationality is a means to better knowledge, whereas postmodernists assume no such thing. Critical theorists see knowledge as a logical outcome of neatly categorized human interests. In other words, they believe that people tend to know about what they are interested in being able to do. Thus, an interest in creating a productive workforce leads us to produce a wealth of knowledge about how to prepare people for various lines of work.

Postmodern theorists see knowledge as tentative, fragmented, multifaceted, and not necessarily rational. Different people hold a variety of perspectives on the same phenomenon for many reasons, not all of them the logical result of any particular interest. One person may view a particular job as a great opportunity whereas another may view it as a demeaning step down. Furthermore, one individual may hold different and even contradictory understandings of a phenomenon at the same time. The same person may consider work both an opportunity and a constraint. A worker may remain in a relatively boring job because it provides the means to pursue an enriching hobby during off-hours, or because there is a wonderful group of coworkers, or because the person anticipates that good performance might lead to more interesting positions in time.

Critical theorists challenge what we think we know is true by demonstrating how it serves the interests of certain individuals and groups at the expense of other individuals and groups. Critical theory is therefore explicitly political and, according to Marx (1983), "the relentless criticism of all existing conditions" (p. 93). Critical theory is an attempt to understand how injustice among people is sustained and reinforced by those who are interested in maintaining power over others, and how emancipatory ideals are thus prevented (Welton, 1995, pp. 12–13).

The German philosopher Jörgen Habermas has been particularly influential among critical theorists of adult learning. Habermas (1972) describes three human interests for which knowledge is developed. Technical interests are those that guide us to control our material environment; technical knowledge is developed to organize and maintain our economic and political systems. As workers, we are interested in acquiring certain skills that are required by the jobs we hold. Practical interests, the second type, are derived from our need to understand one another; this knowledge incorporates our shared meanings in the everyday world of human interaction, or what Habermas calls the *lifeworld*. As members of families, churches, schools, communities, and so forth, we are interested in being able to communicate with one another and live in harmony. Emancipatory interests, the third type, arise from our desire to be free of oppression. Emancipatory knowledge is an understanding of the contradiction between what we know is true or best and how this knowledge can be oppressive when put into practice (Usher, Bryant, and Johnston, 1997). For instance, even though an organization may have a fair and equitable promotion policy on paper, in reality only certain kinds of people may hold positions of power. Inquiry into promotion practices in the interpersonal realm might reveal that managers tend to promote those who are most like them rather than basing their promotion decisions solely on some objective measure of qualifications.

Critical theorists argue that structures of privilege and oppression based on categories like race or ethnicity, gender, class, sexual orientation, physical or mental capability, and age (Tisdell, 1998) are reinforced because the logic that maintains those structures becomes a common-sense lens through which people view and interpret their everyday experiences. Critical theorists often refer to this reinforcing logic as *hegemony*. Hegemony concerns the success of the dominant classes in presenting their definition of reality in such a way that it is accepted by other classes as common sense even though it serves the interests of the dominant classes alone (Giroux, 1997). For instance, Smith (1998) points to a proliferation of standardized tests in public schools and universities. The dominant message is that these tests are objective measures of one's ability to learn. However, tests do not take into account students' different experiences and opportunities to practice, or motivation. Yet new tests are validated by the fact that the same students who achieved high scores on prior tests also receive high scores on the new tests. High scorers continue to be favored throughout their engagement in formal education while low scorers are segregated and labeled as failures.

Learning, then, in the critical worldview, is reflecting on and challenging what we know and how we know it, and perhaps acting to change material and social conditions of oppressed people as well as the commonly held assumptions that reinforce their oppression (Usher, Bryant, and Johnston, 1997; Brookfield, 1993). For example, Quigley and Holsinger (1993) show how favorite adult basic-education texts contain a hidden curriculum promoting "individualism and problem solving in isolation" (p. 26). This message diverts literacy students' attention away from possible systemic explanations of problems (as demonstrated by sexist, racist, and classist stereotypes within the same texts) and community problem solving. Rather, the texts convey a message that deficiencies within individuals are the primary causes of social problems like unemployment and crime. Many stories portray women and people of color as "blissfully helpless within employment and social settings" (p. 27), yet few protagonists in these stories turn to others for help in solving problems. Instead, someone to whom they are subordinate benevolently gives help to them, or they resolve their problems in isolation. Quigley and Holsinger demonstrate that the subtext of literacy texts facilitates the status quo of inequity particularly along race, class, and gender lines. Analyses of these texts result in *emancipatory* knowledge; that is, educators and learners can be freed from the taken-for-granted assumptions about those outside the center—women, people of color, people living in poverty, and so forth—thus opening the way for us to pursue more constructive representations.

Like critical theorists, postmodernists or poststructuralists believe that knowledge is contextual rather than "out there" waiting to be discovered, but they also believe that knowledge is tentative and multifaceted (Bagnall, 1999). Postmodernists believe that since knowledge emerges from a particular context or event, it can shift as quickly as the context shifts, the perspective of the knower shifts, or as events overtake us. Furthermore, unlike critical theorists, postmodernists do not believe that there is any universal rule of democracy or social justice for judging the validity of any expression of knowledge (Usher, Bryant, and Johnston, 1997; Chase, 2000; Pietrykowski, 1996). Postmodern theorists question anything that is presented as knowledge and work toward the inclusion of multiple "truths" in the continued construction of what is known (Tisdell, 1998).

Deconstruction is a powerful postmodern tool for questioning prevailing representations of learners and learning in the adult education literature. The purpose of deconstruction is to identify and discredit the false binaries that structure a communication or "discourse"; that is, to challenge the assertions of what is to be included or excluded as normal, right, or good. Deconstruction does not conclude with a piece of emancipatory knowledge like Quigley and Holsinger's identification of the subtext of literacy books but rather finds meaning continually problematic (Lather, 1991). The ideas or concepts intended to be conveyed in a message are distorted in its construction, communication, and reception: by the language being used, by the culture in which the message is situated, by the audience to which it is directed, by other messages, and by the ways in which messages are perceived (Hart, 1989).

Edwards and Usher (1994), for example, "deconstruct" adult education's understanding of "competence." Competence is defined by most as not only performance of a particular job but the "skills, knowledge and understanding which go into that performance" (p. 7). Knowledge and understanding that do not have anything to do with the performance of a particular job are excluded from discourses of competence. At the same time, there is increasing demand for a flexible workforce with diverse skills, knowledge, and understandings. Thus, a paradox in meaning exists. The discourse of competence in adult education excludes all that is not necessary for the performance of a particular job, yet the discourse in the current workplace requires inclusion of skills, knowledge, and understanding that go beyond particular jobs. In this case, how can we identify what is normal, right, or good?

Power and Learning

It is impossible to regard knowledge from either the critical or postmodern perspectives without considering power. In each worldview, there is a direct link between knowledge and power. Critical theorists tend to see power as a commodity of sorts held by one individual or group over another individual or group. Power tends to flow from a central or higher source like the state, and primarily is exercised by repressing those outside the center (Sawicki, 1991). Knowledge is related to power in the sense that true knowledge can free an individual or group from the oppressive force of power (Usher, Bryant, and Johnston, 1997). Along with the realization that knowledge is created to serve the interests of certain individuals and groups above those of others comes an awareness of one's own ability to participate in the creation of knowledge that serves interests more democratically.

From a postmodern perspective, power is not held by one individual or group but rather is present in the relationships among them (Usher, Bryant, and Johnston, 1997). Anyone can exercise power but no one can possess it; thus it is more appropriately analyzed from the margins or from the bottom up, rather than from the top down (Sawicki, 1991). In any field or discipline, for example, there are normative rules for behavior within that field. At the same time, the field produces active individuals who exert the power necessary to establish, maintain, reinforce, or change the rules (Usher, Bryant, and Johnston, 1997). Power from a postmodern perspective offers both oppressive constraints and productive opportunities. Knowledge and power in postmodernism are intertwined, in that knowledge is an exercise of power (Pietrykowski, 1996), and those with power "know." For example, we "know" that adult learners tend to learn best when their experience is affirmed and built upon (Caffarella, 1994). Yet as Avis (1995) writes, "experience is never innocent" (p. 182). Experience is an accumulation of messages that empower and disempower learners and therefore it must be critiqued. For instance, many of my students come to class with a belief in the efficacy of "getting buy-in" for proposed human resource development (HRD) activities in their work organizations. HRD professionals often use this phrase to describe how they gain cooperation for their ideas from others in their organizations, typically by including those others in planning. Upon critical analysis of real events in their organizations, students come to see that "getting buy-in" frequently has nothing to do with including others in one's decision-making processes but actually involves activities that deceive others into thinking they have a say in decisions when they do not. As experienced by my students in their workplaces, getting buy-in for one's ideas may be effective, but it often does not mean what we say it means.

The character and shape of power and its link to knowledge generally determine how theorists in these two paradigms view learning. Because critical theorists tend to view power as a repressive force reproduced by hegemony, learning is viewed as a process of reflecting on hegemony and replacing it in our consciousnesses with emancipatory knowledge. Furthermore, some critical theorists have argued that individualistic explanations of learning tend to reinforce the status quo; they thus have sought to replace these explanations with group theories of learning. For instance, Finger (1995) argues that increasing individualism in the West makes it much more difficult to work collaboratively on important problems like environmental degradation. He writes that in order to prepare us to form environmental and other problem-solving groups and alliances, adult education's focus should shift from individual learning to "collaborative, vertical, horizontal, and cross-disciplinary learning" (p. 116).

Postmodernists avoid either an individual or a collective focus on learning but rather gaze on the connections between the individual and the social (Tisdell, 1998). Pierre Bourdieu (1990, 1992) concentrates on the tension between the individual and the social with his interrelated concepts of field and *habitus*. The field is analogous to a game, with both explicit and tacit rules of play. All players are "taken in by the game" (Bourdieu and Wacquant, 1992, p. 98) to the extent that they believe in the game and its stakes, and recognize its legitimacy by taking a position in it and competing with other players. Habitus is the internalization of these rules. Habitus is the collection and variety of inclinations individuals have for behaving in acceptable ways within a field (Bourdieu, 1990). For instance, students learn both explicit and tacit rules for expressing themselves in the classroom. Baudelot (1994) finds that one can distinguish "good" university student essays from "poor" ones without looking at the content at all but rather by looking at other characteristics of the papers. Those that receive higher marks tend to have longer sentences and a wealth of vocabulary, among other attributes. Likewise, adult education also has certain rules internalized by theorists within our discipline, like that described by Connelly (1996), who notes that references to Habermas in the literature "no matter how brief or tenuous . . . seem increasingly compulsory if the author is to claim some theoretical validity" (p. 250). Following Bourdieu, writers on adult learning theory incorporate certain theorists, concepts, and language in their texts in order to maintain or gain status and the authority to know. What we know about adult learning is a function of the rules we theorize by.

Like Bourdieu, Foucault (1977, 1980) focuses on fields of power relations, but his treatment of power highlights its fragility. In Bourdieu's model, individuals internalize the dominant messages that perpetuate certain power relations and thus "naturally" act in ways that often reproduce the status quo. Foucault, on the other hand, views these dominant messages, or discourses, as powerful in and of themselves, rather than as facilitators of power. In Foucault's world, power-knowledge—that which is "known" in a particular field—is an expression of power (Edwards and Usher, 1994; Pietrykowski, 1996). Practices based on what Foucault calls power-knowledge are activations of power that may be oppressive or productive, depending on how these pieces of knowledge are brought to bear. Discourse, and therefore power, lies in the hands of no one yet is activated by everyone. Discourse is thus always a site of conflict; it is fragile and requires constant supervision (Preece, 1997). For instance, consider the reclamation of the term "queer." What was formerly a derogatory term is now an expression of political dissidence (Hill, 1995, p. 153). Power is ever-present in the relationships among us and becomes a source of creativity and meaning production when exercised by any learning group, but no one group controls all the power all the time (Inglis, 1997).

Knowledge, Power, and Learning

Critical and postmodern theorists view knowledge, power, and learning differently, as summarized in Table 6.1.

Critical theorists view knowledge as the outcome of human interests. Hegemonic truth claims (claims to know that are accepted as common sense) are subject to challenge when they perpetuate what Lather (1991) calls a "maldistribution" of power. Power, from the critical perspective, is possessed by individuals and groups and exerted upon others through oppressive truth claims. Learning, then, is a process of challenging truth claims and arriving at a critical consciousness that these are not universal truths but claims that serve the interests of some at the expense of others.

Postmodern theorists view knowledge as tentative, multifaceted, and not necessarily rationally connected to any motivation or interest. Truth claims are always subject to challenge, and knowledge is always kept in play rather than concluding on a particular emancipatory note. Knowledge is an

Table 6.1. Comparison of Critical and Postmodern Worldviews

Critical Theory	Postmodernism
Knowledge is a rational product of human interests	Knowledge is tentative, multifaceted, not necessarily rational
Power is possessed by subjects, repressive	Power is expressed by subjects, productive
Knowledge frees subjects from power	Knowledge is an expression of power
Learning is achieved through critical reflection, consciousness raising	Learning is achieved through deconstruction, play, eclecticism

expression of power, which is ever-present but not omnipotent. Learning is a process of continuous deconstruction of knowledge, of playing with contradictions, and of creatively and productively opening the discourse of a field to an eclectic mosaic of many truths.

Theorists with either a critical or postmodern worldview challenge the positivist notion that one can look at but not touch knowledge; that is, can discover knowledge but not have a hand in shaping it. Furthermore, because knowledge is a social product, it is not outside the reach of power and power relations. From either perspective, knowledge is more thoroughly integrated in the *process* and *politics* of learning, rather than being a neutral reward at the end of the learning journey. Learning, then, is not a predictable generic passage, but rather one that can and must be examined for and by many individuals and groups who have many different voices. The most significant contribution to our understanding of adult learning from either the critical or postmodern worldview is the recognition and theoretical inclusion of the diversity of learners we in adult education serve today.

References

Avis, J. "The Validation of Learner Experience: A Conservative Practice?" *Studies in the Education of Adults,* 1995, 27(2), 173–186.

Bagnall, R. G. *Discovering Radical Contingency: Building a Postmodern Agenda in Adult Education.* New York: Peter Lang, 1999.

Baudelot, C. "Student Rhetoric In Exams." In P. Bourdieu, J. Passeron, and M. deSaint Martin (eds.). *Academic Discourse.* Stanford, CA: Stanford University Press, 1994.

Bourdieu, P. B. *The Logic of Practice.* (R. Nice, trans.). Stanford, CA: Stanford University Press, 1990.

Bourdieu, P. B. *The Rules Of Art: Genesis and Structure in the Literary Field.* (S. Emanuel, trans.). Stanford, CA: Stanford University Press, 1992.

Bourdieu, P., and Wacquant, L. *An Invitation to Reflexive Sociology.* Chicago: University of Chicago Press, 1992.

Brookfield, S. "Breaking the Code: Engaging Practitioners in Critical Analysis of Adult Education Literature." *Studies in the Education of Adults,* 1993, 25(1), 64–91.

Caffarella, R. S. *Planning Programs for Adult Learners.* San Francisco: Jossey-Bass, 1994.

Chase, M. "Stories We Tell Them? Teaching Adults History in a Postmodern World." *Studies in the Education of Adults,* 2000, 32(1), 93–106.

Connelly, B. "Interpretations of Jörgen Habermas in Adult Education Writings." *Studies in the Education of Adults,* 1996, 28(2), 241–252.

Edwards, R., and Usher, R. "Disciplining the Subject: The Power of Competence." *Studies in the Education of Adults,* 1994, 26(1), 1–14.

Finger, M. "Adult Education and Society Today." *International Journal of Lifelong Education,* 1995, 14(2), 110–119.

Foucault, M. *Discipline and Punish: The Birth of the Prison.* New York: Vintage Books, 1977.

Foucault, M. *Power/Knowledge: Selected Interviews and Other Writings.* New York: Pantheon Press, 1980.

Giroux, H. A. *Pedagogy and the Politics of Hope: Theory, Culture and Schooling.* Boulder, CO: Westview Press, 1997.

Habermas, J. *Knowledge and Human Interests.* (J. J. Shapiro, trans.). Boston: Beacon Press, 1972.

Hart, R. P. *Modern Rhetorical Criticism*. Glenview, IL: Scott, Foresman and Company, 1989.

Hill, R. J. "Gay Discourse in Adult Education: A Critical Review." *Adult Education Quarterly*, 1995, *45*(3), 142–158.

Inglis, T. "Empowerment and Emancipation." *Adult Education Quarterly*, 1997, *48*(1), 3–17.

Lather, P. *Getting Smart*. New York: Routledge, 1991.

Marx, K. *The Portable Karl Marx*. New York: Penguin Books, 1983.

Pietrykowski, B. "Knowledge and Power in Adult Education: Beyond Freire and Habermas." *Adult Education Quarterly*, 1996, *46*(2), 82–97.

Preece, J. "'Historicity' and Power-Knowledge Games in Continuing Education." *Studies in the Education of Adults*, 1997, *29*(2), 121–136.

Quigley, B. A., and Holsinger, E. "'Happy Consciousness': Ideology and Hidden Curricula in Literacy Education." *Adult Education Quarterly*, 1993 *44*(1), 17–33.

Rosenau, P. M. *Postmodernism and the Social Sciences: Insights, Inroads, and Intrusions*. Princeton, NJ: Princeton University Press, 1992.

Sawicki, J. *Disciplining Foucault: Feminism, Power, and the Body*. New York: Routledge, 1991.

Smith, F. *The Book of Learning and Forgetting*. New York: Teachers College Press, 1998.

Tisdell, E. J. "Poststructural Feminist Pedagogies: The Possibilities and Limitations of Feminist Emancipatory Adult Learning Theory and Practice." *Adult Education Quarterly*, 1998, *48*(3), 139–156.

Usher, R., Bryant, I., and Johnston, R. *Adult Education and the Postmodern Challenge*. New York: Routledge, 1997.

Welton, M. "The Critical Turn in Adult Education Theory." In M. Welton (ed.), *In Defense of the Lifeworld*. Albany, NY: State University of New York Press, 1995, 11–38.

DEBORAH W. KILGORE is assistant professor in educational leadership and policy studies at Iowa State University.

7

Emotions and imagination are integral to the process of adult learning. The imaginal method is discussed as an alternative to rational and reflective processes of meaning-making.

The Power of Feelings: Emotion, Imagination, and the Construction of Meaning in Adult Learning

John M. Dirkx

Recently I participated in a curriculum workshop that focused on developing more contextual, integrated approaches for adult learners. Because I am interested in better understanding how subject matter becomes personally meaningful for adults, I looked forward to this experience with much anticipation and enthusiasm. As the workshop unfolded, however, I found myself growing increasingly dissatisfied and in disagreement with much of what was being said. Group members and the facilitator seemed to be recognizing the importance of contextualizing content and skills within the learners' real-life experiences, but there was a strong, instrumental sense to the ways in which this was being interpreted. I felt myself grow tense. My face felt flushed and it seemed as if a tight knot was forming in the pit of my stomach. I was obviously upset and feeling even a little irritated and angry. I was at a loss as to why I was feeling so strongly about this discussion. My ideas were at odds with the dominant views in the learning group, but why was I reacting so strongly to what was being said? Why should these views of curricular integration evoke such strong emotions and feelings within me? What does this all mean?

This vignette illustrates the powerful role that emotions and feelings can play in otherwise ordinary adult learning experiences. Dominant views of this relationship suggest that emotions are important in adult education because they can either impede or motivate learning. Most of these perspectives inadvertently reinforce a "rationalist doctrine" that pervades most, if not all, formal educational efforts; one that places an emphasis on factual information and the use of reason and reflection to learn from experience.

This chapter presents an alternative way of understanding emotions and adult learning, one that reflects the central role of emotions in our ways of knowing (Heron, 1992). I argue that personally significant and meaningful learning is fundamentally grounded in and is derived from the adult's emotional, imaginative connection with the self and with the broader social world. The meanings we attribute to emotions reflect the particular sociocultural and psychic contexts in which they arise. This process of meaning-making, however, is essentially imaginative and extrarational, rather than merely reflective and rational. Emotionally charged images, evoked through the contexts of adult learning, provide the opportunity for a more profound access to the world by inviting a deeper understanding of ourselves in relationship with it.

Understanding the Meaning and Experience of Emotion in Our Day-to-Day Lives

The expression of emotions within adult learning experiences is not hard to discern. One adult learner described his feelings about returning to school: "I was terrified to death of coming even to this college. . . . the thought just scared the crap out of me." Referring to the first day of class another said, "It's like being scared to death because you know no one. . . . For the people that have been out of school a while and they walk back in here and they know no one, that was like terrifying for me" (Amey and Dirkx, 1999). Contexts for adult learning are also often regarded as "emotional battlegrounds," with learners vying for recognition and authority (Brookfield, 1993). Some learners describe their classroom experiences as boring or stressful while others characterize them as fun and exciting. Some returning adult students look to their classroom experiences as something that connects them more deeply with other learners and the campus (Graham, Donaldson, Kasworm, and Dirkx, 2000). These observations suggest that emotions and feelings play a critical role in our sense of self and in processes of adult learning. As Lupton (1998, p. 6) suggests, "Our concepts of our emotions are often integral to our wider conception of our selves, used to give meaning and provide explanation for our lives."

Understandings of emotion are shaped by specific sociocultural (Denzin, 1984; Hochschild, 1983; Katz, 1999; Lupton, 1998; Lutz, 1988; Lyons, 1995) and psychic contexts (Chodorow, 1999; Chodorow, 1997; Denzin, 1984; Hillman, 1975; Moore, 1992; Ulanov, 1999; Woodman and Dickson, 1996). Through learning and acculturation, we construct the meanings we attribute to emotional states, reflecting "aspects of cultural meaning systems people use in attempting to understand the situations in which they find themselves" (Lutz, 1988, p. 65). The meanings we attribute to emotional states also inform us about ourselves and the broader social world. As Denzin (1984) suggests, "To understand who a person is, it is necessary to understand emotion" (p. 1). Emotions always refer to the self, providing us with a means for developing self-knowledge. They are an integral part of how we interpret and make sense of the day-to-day events in our lives. As we look at and come to understand our sense-making practices in daily life and the ways emotions constitute that practice, we reveal ourselves more fully to ourselves and to others.

Our experience of emotion, however, and our understanding of self arise from more than just rational, conscious thought processes mediated by cultural symbols (Lupton, 1998). As in the opening vignette, we sometimes find ourselves feeling strongly about something or toward someone without really consciously knowing or understanding why or from where these feelings came. Emotional experiences are often shaped by strong inner, extrarational dynamics (Chodorow, 1999). They are not always expressed through words but gain voice in dreams, fantasies, or other imagined aspects of our day-to-day world.

Emotions, then, give voice to our fundamental sense of irrationality (Chodorow, 1999). Through our emotional experiences, we recognize that our conscious sense of agency is often subverted by desire. In these situations, we experience a self that seems ambivalent, contradictory, and fragmented. Our consciousness seems populated by multiple voices, each claiming a different sense of reality (Clark and Dirkx, 2000). Thus, experience of emotion often reveals a multiplistic, contradictory self. For example, I felt angry toward the workshop facilitators, but I also felt guilty for feeling angry at them. Understanding of these multiple selves is achieved not only through conscious, rational, and self-reflexive practices (Mezirow, 1991) but through the products of our imagination, the images that come to populate consciousness (Dirkx, 1998). Relying on Jungian and post-Jungian thought, I now turn to a fuller development of an imaginative view of emotion, and how we might understand its expression in adult learning settings.

Experience of Emotion as Imaginative Engagement

Emotions are often associated with voices or images that emerge within consciousness. As Jung (quoted in Chodorow, 1997, p. 26) suggests, "I learned how helpful it can be . . . to find the particular image which lies behind emotions." Through emotionally charged images, individuals and collectives potentially express and connect with this deeper reality. We use these charged images to perceive and understand ourselves and the world. For example, behind strong feelings of anger and outrage may be a person who feels left out. A sense of confidence within group discussion may be undermined by an image of the imposter lurking at the edges of consciousness. Angry reactions to a teacher may arise from an unconscious image we hold of him or her as an over-controlling parent.

These images convey a deep, inner life constituted by "intentions, behaviors, voices, feelings, that I do not control with my will or cannot connect with my reason" (Hillman, 1975, p. 2). As Whitmont (1969) suggests, "[I]mages may appear spontaneously when inner or outer events which are particularly stark, threatening or powerful must be faced" (p. 74). They are gateways to the unconscious and our emotional, feeling selves, representing deep-seated issues and concerns that may be evoked through our experiences of the world. They connect some aspect of our outer experience with dimly perceived or understood aspects of our inner worlds. Behind the feelings of dissatisfaction, frustration, and anger that I experienced in the curriculum integration workshop was a distinct image that animated my consciousness within this situation. This image can, when properly understood, foster a deeper sense of the underlying meaning that curriculum integration holds for my sense of self within this particular sociocultural context.

Through the formation of images, emotions and feelings express the personal meanings that arise for us within any given context (Chodorow, 1999) and serve to animate our thoughts and actions. These meanings arise through our imaginative connection and engagement with these contexts. Our initial construal of meaning within particular emotional situations is largely an act of fantasy and imagination, guided by our emotional connection with both our inner and outer worlds. They help us understand and make sense of our selves, our relationships with others, and the world we inhabit. Our experience of this inner life is inherently emotional and deeply connected to the sense of self we construct and maintain (Chodorow, 1999; Denzin, 1984; Lupton, 1998). My experience of the workshop was largely mediated by the image that formed within my consciousness. I perceived and interpreted what was happening in this workshop largely through the lens of this image.

Neo- and post-Jungians (Hillman, 1975; Moore, 1992; Sardello, 1992; Ulanov, 1999; Woodman and Dickson, 1996) stress the importance of these emotionally charged images to the vitality and reenchantment of our everyday lives, to fostering our sense of spirituality, and to developing relationships and dialogue with inner selves.

When manifest as images, emotions can be interpreted as "messengers of the soul" (Dirkx, 1997, 1998) seeking to inform us of deeply personal, meaningful connections that are being made within an experience. They are expressions of the deeper, nonegoic aspects of our psyche. Images circumvent the controlling purposes of the ego and put us in touch with a deeper aspect of our being. In her study of personal emotional experiences, Lupton (1998) reported several people who used the concept of soul or spirit to describe the nature of emotions. A thirty-six-year-old woman said of emotions, "I think they're generated, like through your soul. 'Cause I think everybody has a soul and emotion comes from somewhere deep within you and I don't necessarily think it comes from your mind so much. . . . I think it is the soul for me that generates those feelings" (p. 42).

Thus, emotions and our imaginative appraisal of them are integral to the process of meaning-making, to the ways we experience and make sense of ourselves (Campbell, 1997; Chodorow, 1999; Denzin, 1984; Jaggar, 1989) as well as our relationships with others and the world (Damasio, 1994; Goleman, 1995, Harré, 1986; Lupton, 1998). Through the image, emotions help us connect the inner dynamics of the self with the outer objects of our world.

The Connection Between Emotions and Learning in Adulthood

In the *Phaedrus*, Plato described emotions as irrational urges that need to be controlled through the use of reason (Jaggar, 1989) and as major impediments to rationality and the pursuit of truth. This marginalized view of emotions and feelings has continued to the present day. A brief article, on the issue of whether to allow limited use of alcohol at events held at the city zoo, was recently published in the *Lansing State Journal,* a local Michigan newspaper. "Members of the Lansing City Council," the editorial read, "need to reconsider their position that seems based on emotion more than reason. . . . Emotions have thus far ruled the day on this issue. . . . City Council members' obstinate, no-alcohol stance is unreasonable. A little less emotion, if you please, and a lot more reason."

Much of the theory and practice in adult education reveals a similar tradition of marginalizing emotions and elevating rationality to a supreme position. Popular notions frame teaching and learning as largely rational, cognitive processes, and understand emotions as either impediments to or motivators of learning. Reason and rationality are viewed as the primary foundations or processes for learning, through which learners obtain access to the "objective" structures of our world (Jaggar, 1989). Adult educators refer to personal or emotional issues adults bring to the educational setting as "baggage" or "barriers" to learning (Dirkx and Spurgin, 1992; Gray and Dirkx, 2000). Learners seem filled with anxieties or fears (Tennant, 1997). If and when such issues *are* acknowledged by educators, it is often to provide opportunities for learners to "vent" and "get it off their chests" so they can get back to the "business of learning." Educators within formal settings of adult learning seek to control, manage, limit, or redirect outward expressions of emotions and feelings.

On the other hand, many of us implicitly perceive emotional and affective dimensions of learning as also contributing to a positive educational experience. In recalling incidents of memorable learning, participants in the author's teaching-strategies course typically describe experiences in which there was a strong, positive, emotional, or affective dimension, such as a supportive climate, a caring teacher who listens to us as individuals, a teacher who respects us as persons, or a teacher who involves the whole person in the learning experience. Nick, an adult who shared his experiences as a learner with us, said of his teacher, "He just keeps everybody awake. He keeps going and going and going and he comes in with such motivation and enthusiasm. It's like you got no choice but to wanna come to class."

The literature underscores the importance of attending to emotions and feelings in contexts, interactions, and relationships that characterize adult learning (Boud, Cohen, and Walker, 1993; Brookfield, 1993; Daloz, 1986; Postle, 1993; Robertson, 1996; Tennant, 1997). A growing body of research, however, suggests that emotions and feelings are more than merely a motivational concern in learning. Postle (1993) argues that affective, emotional dimensions provide the foundation on which practical, conceptual, and imaginal modes of learning rest. "Brain-based" theories (Damasio, 1994, 1999) and the concept of "emotional intelligence" (Goleman, 1995) suggest that emotion and feelings are deeply interrelated with perceiving and processing information from our external environments, storing and retrieving information in memory, reasoning, and the embodiment of learning (Merriam and Caffarella, 1999; Taylor, 1996). Recent studies of transformative learning reveal extrarational aspects, such as emotion, intuition, soul, spirituality, and the body, as integral to processes of deep, significant change (Clark, 1997; Dirkx, 1997; Nelson, 1997; Scott, 1997).

We are beginning to appreciate the affective and imaginative as modes of knowing in their own right (Heron, 1992; Jaggar, 1989). Imagination plays a key role in connecting our inner, subjective experiences of emotions and feelings with the outer, objective dimensions of our learning experiences. These relationships and dialogues are mediated largely through what Hillman (1975) refers to as "imaginal" approaches, such as dreamwork, free association, fantasy, active imagination, and other forms of creative activity. These approaches bypass ego consciousness and allow for expressions of deeper dimensions of our psychic lives.

Using Images to Make Sense of Feelings and Emotions in Adult Learning

In the presence of powerful emotions and feelings, we make use of images to mediate and construct their meanings. The conscious, purposeful process used to foster this approach is referred to as the "imaginal method" (Hillman, 1975). I will draw on this idea, more a perspective than an actual method, to describe how we might help adults understand and make sense of emotional experiences and feelings that may arise within their learning.

The "text" in adult learning (broadly understood to include print, speech, visual cues, and so on) often evokes emotionally charged images. For example, a middle-aged woman in a course I teach on adult learning was stunned to see her own life so closely described in some of the developmental theories being studied. For years she had felt confused and almost bewildered by certain troubling and painful aspects of her life. Her study of the course text evoked images that suddenly brought all these puzzling experiences into sharp focus. In this new-found self-knowledge, she felt a deep sense of release and joy that she freely shared with her peers.

The images evoked by texts are not merely constructions of our conscious, cognitive egos. Emotionally charged images are not under the willful control of the ego. Rather, they tend to appear spontaneously within the learning process. They arrive as they so choose, as acts of grace, relatively independent of the needs and desires of the ego. Like Marley's ghost in *A Christmas Carol,* these images beckon us to vistas and realms of meaning not open to ordinary, waking, ego-based consciousness. Their presence within the learning context suggests engagement with soul (Dirkx, 1997; Moore, 1992), a deep emotional and spiritual connection between our inner lives and some aspect of our outer experience. Paradoxically, we are more likely to recognize, accept, and actively engage their presence in consciousness when we relax the ego. We often want to make such matters concerns for the ego, but these are ultimately matters of the heart or soul. The harder we try to control this process the more likely soul will go into hiding. It was no accident that Scrooge's ghosts appeared to him in the middle of the night.

The basis for this active engagement and dialogue with our emotions is imagination (Clark, 1997; Nelson, 1997). Imagination helps us connect to and establish a relationship with this powerful, nonegoic aspect of our being (Moore, 1992). By becoming aware of the images behind our emotions and feelings, we connect with the inner forces that populate our psyche. As we learn to participate with them in a more conscious manner, we are less likely to be unwillingly buffeted around by their presence in our lives. Entering into a conscious dialogue with these images creates the opportunity for deeper meaning and more satisfying relationships with our world.

In the imaginal method, we recognize, name, and come to a deeper understanding of the images revealed through our deep, often emotional experiences of the text (Hillman, 1975). Our soul work—our learning—is to recognize, elaborate, and differentiate them as a means of developing a deeper understanding of our experience in the context of adult learning. The purpose of the imaginal method or soul work is not to analyze and dissect these emotions and feelings but to imaginatively elaborate their meaning in our lives. In contrast to Mezirow's (1991) notion of transformative learning, in which we are encouraged to ask "how" or "why" questions about these feelings and emotions, we might simply ask "what": What do these emotions feel like, remind me of? What other times have I felt this way, experienced these emotions? What was going on then? Who was involved in that incident? As we elaborate these feelings and emotions, the nature of the image behind them may begin to emerge. As we recognize, name, and work with these images, we move toward a deeper, more conscious connection with these aspects of ourselves. We befriend that person or persons within our psyche. We transform ordinary existence into the "stuff of soul" (Moore, 1992, p. 205), establishing through imagination a meaningful connection between the text and our life experiences. These emotionally charged images provide access to the psyche, an invitation to the journey of the soul and to coming to know oneself as a more fully individuated being. As they take shape within consciousness, they can deepen our understanding of their meaning. We are allowed to glimpse the nature of soul through the work of the imagination (Hillman, 1989).

Conclusion

I will conclude by briefly illustrating how the imaginal approach helped me develop a more meaningful understanding of my reactions to the curriculum workshop. As I worked with my emotional response to this workshop, I began to see how the idea of integration is, for me, itself an emotionally charged image. On the surface, the *concept* reflects an interest in making learning experiences more meaningful for others. The *image* of integration, however, reflects my deep, underlying orientation to relationships and gives voice to an enduring yearning for wholeness. I now understand that these notions express an aspect of the self searching for wholeness through relationship. In this sense, I imagine instrumental approaches to curriculum as mechanistic, as not honoring my personal search, and ultimately as a denial of this aspect of myself.

The imaginal method seeks a deeper understanding of the emotional, affective, and spiritual dimensions that are often associated with profoundly meaningful experiences in adult learning. Journal writing, literature, poetry, art, movies, story-telling, dance, and ritual are specific methods that can be used to help foster the life of the image in our relationships with adult learners. By approaching emotionally charged experiences imaginatively rather than merely conceptually, learners locate and construct, through enduring mythological motifs, themes, and images, deep meaning, value, and quality in the relationship between the text and their own life experiences.

References

Amey, M., and Dirkx, J. M. "Contextualizing Multiple Life Experiences: Improving Developmental Education." Paper presented at the annual meeting of the Association for the Study of Higher Education (ASHE), San Antonio, TX, November, 1999.

Boud, D., Cohen, R., and Walker, D. "Introduction: Understanding Learning from Experience." In D. Boud, R. Cohen, and D. Walker (eds.), *Using Experience for Learning.* Bristol, PA: Society for Research in Higher Education, 1993.

Brookfield, S. "Through the Lens of Learning: How the Visceral Experience of Learning Reframes Teaching." In D. Boud, R. Cohen, and D. Walker (eds.), *Using Experience for Learning.* Bristol, PA: Society for Research in Higher Education. 1993.

Campbell, S. *Interpreting the Personal: Expression and the Formation of Feelings.* Ithaca, NY: Cornell University Press, 1997.

Chodorow, J. (ed.). *Jung on Active Imagination.* Princeton: Princeton University Press, 1997.

Chodorow, N. *The Power of Feeling: Personal Meaning in Psychoanalysis, Gender, and Culture.* New Haven: Yale University Press, 1999.

Clark, J. E. "Of Writing, Imagination, and Dialogue: A Transformative Experience." In P. Cranton (ed.), *Transformative Learning in Action.* New Directions for Adult and Continuing Education, no.74. San Francisco: Jossey-Bass, 1997.

Clark, M. C., and Dirkx, J. M. "Moving Beyond a Unitary Self: A Reflective Dialogue." In A. Wilson and E. Hayes (eds.), *Handbook of Adult and Continuing Education* (New Edition). San Francisco: Jossey-Bass, 2000.

Daloz, L. D. *Effective Teaching and Mentoring.* San Francisco: Jossey-Bass, 1986.

Damasio, A. R. *Descartes' Error: Emotion, Reason, and the Human Brain.* New York: Avon, 1994.

Damasio, A. R. *The Feeling of What Happens: Body and Emotion in the Making of Consciousness.* New York: Harcourt Brace, 1999.

Denzin, N. *On Understanding Emotion.* San Francisco: Jossey-Bass, 1984.

Dirkx, J. M. "Nurturing Soul in Adult Learning." In P. Cranton, (ed.), *Transformative Learning in Action.* New Directions for Adult and Continuing Education, no.74. San Francisco: Jossey-Bass, 1997.

Dirkx, J. M. "Knowing the Self Through Fantasy: Toward a Mytho-Poetic View of Transformative Learning." In J. C. Kimmel (ed.), *Proceedings of the 39th Annual Adult Education Research Conference.* San Antonio, TX: University of Incarnate Word and Texas A&M University, 1998.

Dirkx, J. M., and Spurgin, M. E. "Implicit Theories of Adult Basic Education Teachers: How Their Beliefs About Students Shape Classroom Practice." *Adult Basic Education,* 1992, 2(1), 20–41.

Goleman, D. *Emotional Intelligence.* New York: Bantam Books, 1995.

Graham, S. W., Donaldson, J.F., Kashorn, C., and Dirkx, J. "The Experiences of Adult Undergraduates—What Shapes Their Learning?" Presented at the Annual Meeting of the American Educational Research Association, New Orleans, LA: April 24–28, 2000 (ED 440275).

Gray, J. E., and Dirkx, J. M. "The Good, the Bad, and the Struggling: Beliefs About Student Preparedness Among Teachers in an Adult Learning College." In proceedings of the 19th Midwest Research-to-Practice Conference in Adult, Continuing, and Community Education. Madison, WI: University of Wisconsin, 2000.

Harré, R. (ed.). *The Social Constructions of Emotions.* Oxford: Basil Blackwell, 1986.

Heron, J. *Feeling and Personhood: Psychology in Another Key.* London: Sage, 1992.

Hillman, J. *Re-visioning Psychology.* New York: HarperCollins, 1975.

Hillman, J. "The Poetic Basis of Mind." In T. Moore (ed.), *A Blue Fire: Selected Writings by James Hillman.* New York: HarperCollins, 1989.

Hochschild, A. *The Managed Heart: Commercialization of Human Feeling.* Berkeley, CA: University of California Press, 1983.

Jaggar, A. "Love and Knowledge: Emotion in Feminist Epistemology." *Inquiry,* 1989, 32, 151–76.

Katz, J. *How Emotions Work.* Chicago: University of Chicago Press, 1999.

Lupton, D. *The Emotional Self: a Socio-cultural Exploration.* Thousand Oaks: Sage, 1998.

Lutz, C. *Unnatural Emotions: Everyday Sentiments on a Micronesian Atoll and Their Challenges to Western Theory.* Chicago: University of Chicago Press, 1988.

Lyons, M. "Missing Emotion: The Limitations of Cultural Constructionism in the Study of Emotion." *Cultural Anthropology,* 1995, 10(2), 44–26.

Merriam, S. B., and Caffarella, R. S. *Learning in Adulthood: A Comprehensive Guide.* (2nd Ed.). San Francisco: Jossey-Bass, 1999.

Mezirow, J. *Transformative Dimensions of Adult Learning.* San Francisco: Jossey-Bass, 1991.

Moore, T. *Care of the Soul: A Guide for Cultivating Depth and Sacredness in Everyday Life.* New York: HarperCollins, 1992.

Nelson, A. "Imaging and Critical Reflection in Autobiography: An Odd Couple in Adult Transformative Learning." In R. E. Nolan and H. Chelesvig (eds.), *38th Annual Adult Education Research Conference Proceedings.* Stillwater, OK: Oklahoma State University, 1997.

Postle, D. "Putting Heart Back into Learning." In D. Boud, R. Cohen, and D. Walker (eds.), *Using Experience for Learning.* Bristol, PA: Society for Research in Higher Education, 1993.

Robertson, D. L. (1996). "Facilitating Transformative Learning: Attending to the Dynamics of the Educational Helping Relationship." *Adult Education Quarterly,* 1996, 47(1), 41–53.

Sardello, R. *Facing the World with Soul: The Reimagination of Modern Life.* New York: HarperPerennial, 1992.

Scott. S. M. "The Grieving Soul in the Transformative Process." In P. Cranton (ed.), *Transformative Learning in Action.* New Directions for Adult and Continuing Education, no. 74. San Francisco: Jossey-Bass, 1997.

Taylor, E. W. "Rationality and Emotions in Transformative Learning: A Neurobiological Perspective." *Proceedings of the Adult Education Research Conference,* 37. Tampa: University of South Florida, 1996.

Tennant, M. *Psychology and Adult Learning.* (2nd Ed.). London: Routledge, 1997.

Ulanov, A. B. *Religion and the Spiritual in Carl Jung.* New York: Paulist Press, 1999.

Whitmont, E. C. *The Symbolic Quest: Basic Concepts of Analytical Psychology.* Princeton: Princeton University Press, 1969.

Woodman, M., and Dickson, E. *Dancing in the Flames: The Dark Goddess in the Transformation of Consciousness.* Boston: Shambala, 1996.

JOHN M. DIRKX *is associate professor of higher and adult education and codirector of the Michigan Center for Career and Technical Education at Michigan State University.*

8

New knowledge of the brain and consciousness can be
used to understand adult learning and develop new
principles for adult education.

The Brain and Consciousness: Sources of Information for Understanding Adult Learning

Lilian H. Hill

More is known about the brain than ever before, with more yet to be discovered. Educators are just beginning to learn how new knowledge of the brain can be applied to enhance learning for people of all ages. This chapter describes current knowledge of the brain and consciousness and concludes with how this knowledge affects our understanding of adult learning.

The Neurobiology of the Brain

The brain weighs a mere three pounds and consists of approximately 100 billion interconnected cells, forming "an immensely complicated, intricately woven tissue" composed of highly specialized nerve cells or neurons (Parnavelas, 1998). These cells are connected by synapses numbering more than 10,000 times their number.

In the embryonic stage of development, nerve cells in the brain proliferate rapidly, beginning with just a few cells at conception to 200 billion cells in a few months. Approximately 50 percent of these neurons fail to form connections with other parts of the body and die. Twenty weeks after conception, the brain is organized into forty different physical maps governing activities such as vision, muscle movement, and hearing. The basis of language, vision, thinking, and the personality are in place. The architecture of the brain has been created (Kotulak, 1997).

After the framework of the brain is established, the experiences a person has and the environment he or she lives in are influential in shaping the brain. The brain takes in information from the outside world through the sensory organs and fashions a mental map. The brain is constantly in a state of growth or reorganization, and depends on a stimulating environment, which is particularly important in childhood. For example, if vision is blocked in infancy, neurons that would have been devoted to vision are permanently diverted to other functions. For this reason, cataracts that block vision in newborns are now removed within a few days so that normal vision is able to develop (Kotulak, 1997; Ornstein, 1991).

The structure of the brain is also influenced by hormones, especially sex hormones. The right and left brain have their greatest growth and appear to become specialized at the same time that the sex hormones come into play (Kotulak, 1997). Female brains differ from male brains in several significant ways (Jensen, 1996). Some examples of these differences include the length of nerve cell receptors, pathways the nerves follow, and location of control centers for language, emotion, and spatial skills. Female brains are more responsive to emotional stimulation than male brains (Blum, 2000). Male brains tend to be 15 percent larger, but no link to intelligence or body size has been determined. Female brains retain flexibility longer than male brains and are not as subject to degeneration until later in life. Despite documented differences in male and female brains, Jensen (1996) cautions that culturally held stereotypes should be avoided and that every person needs to be encouraged to develop in ways that builds on his or her individual strengths.

Structure and Functions of the Brain. Efforts to physically map the brain have correlated more than forty brain functions with different locations (Greenfield, 1997). The use of imaging techniques such as CT Scans and Magnetic Resonance Imaging (MRI) reveals that different regions of the brain work in a coordinated fashion to accomplish different tasks. Some authors suggest it is more useful to think of brain processes rather than the locations of those processes.

Brain functions involve the flow of information through complex networks of nerve cells in the brain and the body. Information is transferred from one neuron to another at synapses, junctions that form points of contact. A single neuron can have from a few thousand up to one hundred thousand synapses, and each synapse can receive information from thousands of other neurons. The resulting 100 trillion synapses make possible the complex cognition of human learners (Parnavelas, 1998).

Communication between neurons is accomplished through both chemical and electrical signals. When a neuron is activated it produces electrical impulses that interact with other nerve cells. Neurotransmitters such as serotonin are released that readily bind with receptor molecules. The diversity of more than fifty neurotransmitters is thought to permit a "rich grammar of interactions between neurons" that facilitates a wide range of responses in differing situations (Robbins, 1998, p. 35).

Neuroflexibility. The adult brain is much more flexible than the rigid structure it was once believed to be. For the duration of the life span the brain continues to change and reorganize in response to environmental stimulation. The brain "is not a static organ; it is a constantly changing mass of cell connections that are deeply affected by experience and hold the key to human intelligence" (Kotulak, 1997, p. 13). This is known as *neuroflexibility* or *neuroplasticity*. The most flexible parts of the brain involve higher functions evolved in the cerebral cortex such as thought, memory, and learning. (Dowling, 1998).

The brain tends to habitually and selectively attend to information, resulting in neural pruning (Cardillichio and Field, 1997). Neural branching, in which more connections between neurons develop, can be stimulated by questioning strategies that encourage divergent thinking. Inviting students to analyze the complex set of circumstances that make up an event or phenomenon, for example, can overcome our brain's tendency to simplify events.

Learning and Memory. Biochemical change "at the receptor level is the molecular basis of memory" (Pert, 1997, p. 143). Long-term memory appears to be situated in the hippocampus, a brain structure located deep in the midbrain (Dowling, 1998). People with brain injuries in this area have little ability to remember events for more than a few minutes. A patient whose doctors removed the hippocampus to relieve severe epilepsy displayed this disability. This phenomenon has prompted the idea that long-term memories may be formed in the hippocampus but are transferred elsewhere in the brain for long-term storage (Dowling, 1998).

Learning and memory are context driven. Our brain sorts information depending on whether it is associated with content or context. Content information is usually driven by rote learning, and Jensen (1996) asserts that this kind of learning is not brain-compatible and requires people to employ intense, continuous effort to keep their knowledge fresh. Context-driven learning seems effortless by comparison. This more brain-friendly kind of learning forms quickly, is easily updated, and has almost unlimited capacity. Jensen is not advocating that rote learning be entirely abandoned, simply that we supplement it with activities that help people recall new information.

We remember better when we are exposed to stimulation that engages multiple brain functions. For example, being asked to analyze a word results in stronger memories of it than simply being asked to memorize it (Fishback, 1998/1999). For best recall, multiple sensory experiences should be employed to encode memory with vision, hearing, sound, smell, or movement, and relationships.

Extended, extreme stress can alter brain function in the hippocampus, actually shrinking its size, thereby diminishing the brain's ability to remember experiences (Fishback, 1998/1999). Long-term depression also has a negative impact on learning and may indicate decreased brain activity in the hippocampus, impeding memory (Dowling, 1998). Memory loss associated with severe depression may be related to a failure to attend to new experiences or a failure to create new memories (Singh Kalsa, 1997).

Emotions and Learning. Evolutionary processes have preserved emotional feelings for an important purpose, our survival. Emotions such as fear or love prompt self-preserving actions such as running from a predator or seeking a mate. Emotions also help to prepare people for physical reactions needed in specific situations. For example, when a person needs to flee, increased oxygen and blood flow will be sent to the legs without conscious thought (Damasio, 1999).

Emotions are vital to thought and to learning. The body, emotions, brains, and mind form an integrated system (Damasio, 1999; Pert, 1997), and emotions are enmeshed in neural networks involving reason. Brain damage affecting the emotions impedes judgment and decision making. Emotions increase the strength of memories and help to recall the context of an experience, rendering it meaningful. Emotion, thoughts, and memory are closely interrelated and cannot be separated (LeDoux, 1996).

The Aging Brain. The notion that the brain becomes less flexible for learning as we age has been overturned. Autopsy studies show that brains of university graduates have up to 40 percent more connections than those of high-school dropouts (Kotulak, 1997). However, graduates whose lives were relatively unstimulating after they concluded their studies lost many of the connections formed during their postsecondary education.

We remember what we believe is significant is an idea that can help aging baby-boomers adjust to diminishing abilities to remember details. Age-associated memory impairment affects most people and can be observed by the fifth decade. Older brains are not quite as good as infant brains at mental repair and some functions do slow down (Kotulak, 1997). Aging brains still perform an amazing job of rewiring, as can be observed in people who recover mental and physical function after a stroke. If an area of the brain is permanently damaged, very often responsibility for that function is simply rerouted to another part of the brain; new brain connections are made. This process depends on time and stimulation, whether that be physical therapy or mental exercise.

Age-related cognitive problems are caused by various factors including impaired blood circulation and decreased amounts of neurotransmitters circulating throughout the body. Biological depression, extended stress, and chronic illness can cause cognitive deterioration. Decreasing levels of estrogen associated with age has an impact on our abilities to form new memories. Four factors help to retain mental agility: (1) education, (2) strenuous activity, (3) adequate lung function, and (4) the absence of chronic disease (Singh Kalsa, 1997). Much like the body, the brain requires exercise to remain healthy (Dowling, 1998; Kotulak, 1997). Participation in stimulating activities like reading, travel, cultural events, and social groups assists people in remaining mentally acute. High levels of education and a complex, stimulating lifestyle help in retaining high cognitive function.

Our neural networks have the potential to become more sophisticated as we age (Fishback, 1998/1999). By keeping mentally active, we form new brain connections. Older people may not do this as quickly as before, but they make up for it by having more experience to which to connect new events. Young people perform better on tests requiring rote memorization, displaying *fluid intelligence* based in quick processing skills. The advantage age confers is *crystallized intelligence,* which depends on the richness of accumulated life experience, well-developed verbal abilities, and judgement (Carper, 2000).

The Mind and Consciousness

The mind and consciousness may be emergent properties of the brain (Horgan, 1999), but how the brain constructs the mind or consciousness is not well understood. Damasio (1999) believes that mind is a process that "encompasses both conscious and unconscious operations" (p. 337). In contrast, consciousness is "an entirely private, first-person phenomenon which occurs" as part of what we call mind (p. 12). Mind involves intelligence and the faculties of thought, reasoning, and intelligence. Consciousness refers to the ability to be self-aware and make meaning of our experiences.

Consciousness can also be thought of as a sense of identity, especially the complex attitudes, beliefs, and sensitivities held by an individual (Buncombe, 1995). Pinker (1997) describes both self-knowledge and sentience as parts of consciousness. McKenzie (1991) indicates that there are two forms of consciousness, one based in sensate data and the other involved with constructing meaning. Awareness of sensory knowledge is a consequence of being alive. The second form of consciousness involves investing selected sensory data with meaning; it involves abstract notions of thinking.

Damasio (1999) describes two levels of consciousness, beginning with core consciousness characterized by wakefulness, background emotion, and low-level attention. Awareness of events in core consciousness is transient, while the second level, extended consciousness, integrates these events within an individual history consisting of past, present, and anticipated future events. The creation of this autobiographical self depends on substantial memory capacity and the ability to learn. Consciousness involves the generation of a sense of self and is an essential component of intelligence. It is an innate capacity, but one significantly influenced by culture.

Hayward (1999) critiques the way that consciousness is reduced to brain function in most scientific research. He suggests that between physical matter and the sacred are a spectrum of levels of energy. This energy is characterized not merely as physical energy, but as psycho/spiritual/material energy. In other words, people do not exist only on the individual physical level, but also in connection with each other and the spiritual. Human development occurs not only in the personal but also in the universal, spiritual dimension (Miller, 1999).

This concept resonates with Carl Jung's description of the collective unconscious. He describes the human psyche as having three levels: the conscious, the personal unconscious consisting of forgotten or repressed experiences, and the collective unconscious, which consists of a "collective, universal, and impersonal nature which is identical in all individuals" (Jung, 1968, p. 43). Images in the collective unconscious are not based in personal experience but are inherited. Personal unconscious is held near the surface of the conscious mind, but the collective unconscious exists at a much deeper level in the psyche and may not come to consciousness except in dreams. Despite this, consistent motifs may be found across cultures.

Discussions of human consciousness taking place in other disciplines including psychology, philosophy, and recently education tackle the difficult problem of understanding and relating our individual experiences to that of others and to societal understandings of reality (Midgely, 1998). Wilson (1998) indicates that culture is "created by the communal mind" and that the "mind grows from birth to death by absorbing parts of the existing culture available to it" (p. 138). Culture is recreated collectively in the minds of individuals, and this relationship is dynamic, meaning that cultures adapt to changing circumstances.

Each culture shares a common worldview that affects the consciousness of people and their relationships. Western culture appears to be growing away from an industrial, scientific worldview that emphasizes materialism, competition, and individualism. The emerging paradigm is characterized by (1) a more inclusive worldview and the formation of allegiances beyond the local, (2) an awareness of interdependence among humans and between humankind and the earth, (3) an ability to cope comfortably with ambiguity, and (4) a valuing of complexity and diversity. This developing global consciousness (Hill, 1998) involves changes in the way we think and in our relationships with the earth and people worldwide.

Harman (1998) charts a new societal course that is developing in reaction to the consequences of the industrial, scientific, and especially economic paradigm that dominates the global economy and acts to suppress other societal beliefs. Mental characteristics integral to global mind change include "a search for wholeness, search for community and relationship, search for identity, search for meaning, and sense of empowerment" (p. 133). O'Sullivan (1999) believes that the "fundamental educational task of our time is to make the choice for a sustainable planetary habitat" (p. 2). Our educational systems must be based on a transformative vision that sees ourselves as one with the wider community of the earth.

What Does this Mean for Adult Learning?

The knowledge we now have about the brain dispels forever the notion that adults have difficulty learning. Principles of learning grounded in brain and consciousness research are being developed that inform adult education practice. Several are discussed below.

People's experiences differ and so do their brains.   Each brain is unique because experience affects the creation and architecture of the brain. Individuals become more diverse as they mature since experiences and the neural connections people make are distinctive.

The concept of neuroflexibility reinforces lifelong learning.   In healthy individuals, aging does not diminish adults' capacity for learning. The brain requires mental exercise and exposure to novel experiences throughout life to remain vital.

Information that is contextually embedded is easier to learn.   The brain is not skilled in learning isolated, sequential bits of information but very quick to learn in situations that are true to real life. Contextual memory refers to information associated with circumstances, locations, and emotions. Adult education research in situated cognition and contextual learning offers valuable insights to draw on.

Emotional states are the link between learning and memory.   They are intertwined with reasoning and decision-making. We literally must feel something is true before it can be believed and learned. Positive emotions allow people to recall experiences with greater clarity.

Employing multiple sensory experiences helps to activate learning.   Learning is activated by creating different pathways in the brain that are engaged in memory of new material. The brain operates simultaneously on many levels in a coordinated fashion. This tendency can be utilized in the classroom since memory and learning are stimulated by experiences involving different senses and relationships.

Learning involves the creation of meaning.   In order to make meaning of new information, the brain will connect new experiences to previous ones activating consciousness. Assisting students in connecting learning experiences to their personal lives helps them to learn in ways that are relevant.

Discussion of values and adult students' concerns for the world around them connect our experiences to the world.   The way we teach and learn affects the world around us. Ideally, adult education helps adults develop their potential so that "the learners become more liberated as adults, better capacitated to participate in the lives of their communities and institutions, and empowered to create an authentically human future" (McKenzie, 1991, p. 129).

In summary, knowledge of the brain and consciousness provides a basis for better understanding adult learning. The most exciting discovery is the brain's tremendous plasticity, its ability to respond to learning throughout life. Emotional states and sensory experiences are integrally involved in learning.

Consciousness integrates personal experiences, making new learning relevant. Finally, meaning, values, and people's relationships with others, their communities, and the world around them are essential to adult learning.

References

Blum, D. "Unraveling the Mysteries of Man vs. Woman." *Georgia Magazine,* 2000, 76(3), 12–27.

Buncombe, M. *The Substance of Consciousness: An Argument of Interactionism.* Brookfield, VT: Aldershot, 1995.

Cardillichio, T., and Field, W. "Seven Strategies That Encourage Neural Branching." *Educational Leadership,* 1997, 54(6), 33–36.

Carper, J. *Your Miracle Brain.* New York: HarperCollins, 2000.

Damasio, A. *The Feeling of What Happens: Body and Emotion in the Making of Consciousness.* New York: Harcourt Brace, 1999.

Dowling, J. E. *Creating Mind: How the Brain Works.* New York: Norton, 1998.

Fishback, S. J. "Learning and the Brain." *Adult Learning,* 1998/1999, 10(2), 18–22.

Greenfield, S. A. *The Human Brain: A Guided Tour.* New York: Basic Books, 1997.

Harman, W. *Global Mind Change: The Promise of the 21st Century* (2nd ed.). San Francisco: Berrett-Koehler, 1998.

Hayward, J. "Unlearning to See the Sacred." In S. Glazer (ed.), *The Heart of Learning: Spirituality in Education.* New York: Jeremy P. Tarcher/Putnam, 1999.

Hill, L. H. (1998). "Changes of the Human Mind." *Adult Education Quarterly,* 1998, 49(1), 56–64.

Horgan, J. *The Undiscovered Mind: How the Human Brain Defies Replication, Medication, and Explanation.* New York: Free Press, 1999.

Jensen, E. *Brain-Based Learning.* Del Mar, CA: Turning Point, 1996.

Jung, C. G. *The Archetypes and the Collective Unconscious.* (3rd ed.) Princeton, NJ: Princeton University Press, 1968.

Kotulak, R. *Inside the Brain: Revolutionary Discoveries of How the Brain Works.* Kansas City, KS: Andrews McMeel, 1997.

LeDoux, J. *The Emotional Brain: The Mysterious Underpinnings of Emotional Life.* New York: Simon & Schuster, 1996.

McKenzie, L. *Adult Education and Worldview Construction.* Malabar, FL: Krieger, 1991.

Midgely, M. "One World, But a Big One." In S. Rose (ed.), *From Brains to Consciousness?* Princeton, NJ: Princeton University Press, 1998.

Miller,, R. "Holistic Education for an Emerging Culture." In S. Glazer (ed.), *The Heart of Learning: Spirituality in Education.* New York: Jeremy P. Tarcher/Putnam, 1999.

Ornstein, R. *Evolution of Consciousness: The Origins of the Way We Think.* New York: Simon & Schuster, 1991.

O'Sullivan, E. *Transformative Learning: Educational Vision for the 21st Century.* London: Zed Books, 1999.

Parnavelas, J. "The Human Brain: 100 Billion Connected Cells." In S. Rose (ed.), *From Brains to Consciousness?* Princeton, NJ: Princeton University Press, 1998.

Pert, C. *Molecules of Emotion: The Science Behind Mind-Body Medicine.* New York, Simon & Schuster, 1997.

Pinker, S. *How the Mind Works.* New York: Norton, 1997.

Robbins, T. "The Pharmacology of Thought and Emotion." In S. Rose (ed.), *From Brains to Consciousness?* Princeton, NJ: Princeton University Press, 1998.

Singh Kalsa, D. *Brain Longevity: Regenerate Your Concentration, Energy, and Learning Ability for a Lifetime of Peak Mental Performance.* New York: Warner Books, 1997.

Wilson, E. O. *Consilience: The Unity of Knowledge.* New York: Random House, 1998.

LILIAN H. HILL is education specialist and assistant professor at Virginia Commonwealth University in Richmond, Virginia.

9

This chapter explores somatic learning and narrative learning, two lesser-known but valuable ways in which adults learn.

Off the Beaten Path: Some Creative Approaches to Adult Learning

M. Carolyn Clark

This journal is like a hike across the varied terrain of adult learning theory. It begins on level ground with the wide and well-traveled path of models of learning that essentially defined us as a field early on, moves on to a somewhat steeper grade of the currently fashionable and often challenging modes of learning, then winds through the forest of more complex, interdisciplinary approaches. With this chapter we're on the other side of the forest, confronting an immense prairie of tall grass and big sky; the recognizable path has dissolved into a labyrinth of rabbit trails leading off in multiple directions. Where to now??

The truth is that out here on the prairie there are lots of possibilities, and the direction you choose is determined more by personal predilection than current fashion. When I say these types of learning are off the beaten path of adult education, I mean that they are topics that we rarely encounter in our own journals and conferences. However, our field has always been interdisciplinary, some would say eclectic, so explorations of this sort are quite normal for us. This chapter, then, simply presents areas that intrigue me at the moment; others would make different choices, I'm sure.

I've chosen two types of learning. The literature on both of these areas is usually framed in terms of knowing, but here I will use the terms knowing and learning somewhat interchangeably. The first type is the connection between learning and the body, what is usually called somatic learning. While we know a fair amount about kinesthetic learning and physical skill development, we know little about how we learn from our bodily experience. The second area that intrigues me is narrative learning. Here I'm curious about how the narrative process itself—the storying of our experience—teaches us something.

NEW DIRECTIONS FOR ADULT AND CONTINUING EDUCATION, no. 89, Spring 2001 © Jossey-Bass, A Publishing Unit of John Wiley & Sons, Inc.

Both types of learning cover a lot of ground. My plan for this chapter is to describe the fundamental concepts of each type of learning, discuss a few specific examples of how that learning is manifested, and briefly explore how these modes of learning might influence our practice as adult educators.

Somatic or Embodied Learning

Years ago I had a friend who was studying art, and one of her assignments was to do a self-portrait. The other students drew their faces; my friend drew her body. I was jolted by her portrait because, like the other students, I identify my self with my head and not my body. This isn't surprising because we're situated within a culture that has a complex and largely troubled relationship with the body. The Western cultural discourse on the body is couched most often in terms of gaining control over it, most prominently by physical exercise or by dieting, so that we can meet social norms of healthiness or body size. But short of the assaults of illness and aging, our experience of the body is usually unconscious and largely unspoken. We live much more comfortably in our heads than in our bodies.

Things were not always this way. In medieval times, knowing was more emotional, more internal, more connected to the natural world (Bordo, 1987). Berman (1989) makes the case that the senses were primary in this period, that "'the facts' were first and foremost what happened on a psychic and emotional level" rather than being determined through the exercise of reason, and that "the essential truth was an interior one" (p. 111). A person "knew" something by being deeply and intimately connected to it, a knowing that was somatic and emotional.

With the rise of the Scientific Revolution, beginning especially with Descartes, this interior knowing through a sense of connectedness was displaced by the primacy of reason and the requirement that the knower and the known be separate and distinct. In privileging reason, the body is delegitimated as a mode of knowing. Bordo (1987) notes that there are two dimensions to the Cartesian worldview:

> On the one hand, a new model of knowledge is conceived, in which the purity of the intellect is guaranteed through its ability to transcend the body. On the other hand . . . the spiritual and the corporeal are now two distinct substances which share no qualities (other than being created), permit of interaction but no merging, and are each defined precisely in opposition to the other [p. 99].

The consequence of this split is that the primary way of knowing the world in the modern era has been cognitive. "Somatic and emotional knowing, then, came to be regarded as unreliable, biased, and 'only' subjective, a mode of knowing that may be useful for our intimate, personal lives, but not for claiming knowledge about the world" (Heshusius and Ballard, 1996, p. 5).

In recent years we've seen renewed legitimization of the body. Much of this work has been located within the Women's Movement, since one means by which women have been disempowered and marginalized in our culture is by associating them with the body. In consciousness-raising groups, issues related to the regulation of their bodies and their sexuality were addressed by women as part of their reflection on their oppression. What had been considered secret and even shameful began to be the object of study and public discourse. Feminist scholars began to theorize the body as foundational for women's conceptualization of the self and the construction of knowledge (see, for example, Jaggar and Bordo, 1989). And perhaps even more important, many popular women writers began to speak honestly about their experience, including their bodily experience.

My personal favorite in the last category is Nancy Mairs (1990). She writes with refreshing frankness about her own experience with multiple sclerosis. In recounting the development of her disease, she says the hardest part has been "the fact that it has rammed my 'self' straight back into the body I had been trained to believe it could, through high-minded acts and aspirations, rise above" (p. 84). And it's a body that she talks about honestly and without shame: "No more lithe, girlish figure: my belly sags from loss of muscle tone, which also creates all kinds of intestinal disruptions, hopelessly humiliating in a society in which excretory functions remain strictly unspeakable. No more sex, either, if society had its way. . . . Fortunately, I've got a husband with a strong libido and a weak sense of social propriety" (pp. 89–90). It is precisely this willingness to give voice to what our culture tells us to shroud in silence that creates freedom, bringing the body "into the plain light of shared human experience" (p. 92).

With greater freedom to speak honestly about the body comes growing awareness of how the body is a source of knowledge. All of us, of course, have the experience of stress manifesting itself in our bodies before our heads fully understand what trouble we're in. That in itself is an example of how we tend to discount somatic knowing in our everyday experience. Polanyi (1969), in his work on tacit knowing, argues that knowledge actually begins in the body: "Every time we make sense of the world, we rely on our tacit knowledge of impacts made by the world on our body and the complex responses of our body to these impacts. Such is the exceptional position of our body in the universe" (p. 147–148). In a sense we lead with our body.

Michelson (1998) offers an interesting example of this in her discussion of experiential learning. Ironically, the traditional understanding of experiential learning has been cognitive—we have an experience, then later we reflect on it. This locates the learning in the act of reflection rather than in the experience itself. Michelson argues that the body needs to be understood as the site of learning. To illustrate this she tells a story about Mary, a manager who has just been promoted to the position of team director. In their first team meeting, one of the senior men acts dismissively to the more junior women, then later claims their ideas as his own. Mary notices this, is angered by it, but chooses not to confront the behavior in the meeting. Tense and agitated, she gets on the train to go home after work and there reflects on the experience and figures out some strategies to deal with the problem. Michelson argues that Mary's learning happened at the meeting, not on the train:

> The understanding that came to Mary on the way home was not a cognitive flash of new learning, but simply the moment in which her mental processes caught up with what her body already knew. . . . Thus, her learning is understood as a moment of emotional and physical response, not a moment of dispassionate self-reflection, as the product of an embodied, social selfhood rather than of a disembodied mind [p. 226].

Michelson isn't saying that the cognitive dimension here is unimportant, but she is making a case, and I think a persuasive one, for the legitimation of somatic learning.

Heshusius and Ballard (1996) offer a different example that makes this point. They examine the stories of scholars who made the shift from positivism to interpretivism as their paradigm of research. This, of course, is a very intellectual process, one that involves examining assumptions about reality and the process of knowing, yet they and the other scholars they studied did not come to their new positions solely through the application of reason. Instead, each of them began with an inner sense, a gut sense, that they needed to change. Heshusius and Ballard describe their own experience that gave rise to their book:

> When we started to consciously reflect on how we had changed our most basic beliefs, we had to acknowledge that we knew, before we could account for it intellectually, that we no longer believed in what we were doing or in what we were being taught. That is, while the dominant assumptions still made sense rationally in terms of how things are done, they no longer made sense somatically and affectively. Something *felt* wrong. Our bodies told us so [1996, p. 2].

How can this notion of somatic knowing be used in an educational context? Matthews (1998) considers this form of knowing to be "at the heart of the arts and applied culture and is at least as central to daily competence as the analytically discursive, distanced knowing that traditional schools cultivate. . . . [it is] the embodied experience of being and doing" (p. 237). He tells the story of his fifth-grade teacher, who excited her students about science by giving them lab coats and inviting them to "*become* scientists" as they did the things scientists do—apply all their senses to the world around them and try to make sense of it. It is this act of embodiment that engages students most completely in the learning process. Crowdes' (2000) sociology students studied power relations by physically engaging in several exercises and then reflecting on their somatic and emotional responses to the experience. For example, in one exercise students were paired up and then faced each other across a line on the floor, with the objective of getting their partner on their side of the line. It was their full experiencing of pushing, arguing, resisting, and occasionally cooperating (simply trading places would make both win) that enabled them to better understand how power works. These examples suggest how powerful somatic learning can be. They also illustrate the creativity that is necessary to facilitate learning in this way.

Narrative Learning

When we think of narrative we typically think of stories, accounts of events that happened to us or to others, real or imagined. It is probably through the examination of our own stories that we can begin to understand the underlying purpose of narrative, which is to enable us to make sense of our experience. Because we are instinctive storytellers, this is a fundamental mode of meaning-making. Bruner (1986) goes so far as to claim that narrative is one of two modes of thought (the other being scientific—what he terms "paradigmatic") and that "it deals in human . . . intention and action and the vicissitudes and consequences that mark their course" (p. 13). This function of narrative to deal with what is most human is especially obvious when we are confronted with tragedy. Riessman (1993, p. 4) quotes Isak Dinesen as saying, "All sorrows can be borne if we can put them into a story." But narrative really suffuses all aspects of our lives.

Narrative is closely linked to our understanding of ourselves. As Rosenwald and Ochberg (1992, p. 1) argue, "Personal stories are not merely a way of telling someone (or oneself) about one's life; they are the means by which identities may be fashioned." Rossiter (1999) thinks of the self as "an unfolding story" in that "as we understand the world and our experiences narratively, so also do we understand and construct the self as narrative" (p. 62). That construction is complex and ongoing, but the central task of the personal narrative is the creation of coherence. Our lives need to make sense, to have their various elements be in a reasonable relationship with one another. Linde (1993) makes the point that coherence has two elements: continuity and causality. She notes that the most common mode of continuity is the identity of the self across time. Gergen and Gergen (1988) go a bit further, seeing continuity as a process by which "the individual attempts to understand life events as systematically related. . . . [so that] one's present identity is thus not a sudden and mysterious event, but a sensible result of a life story" (p. 19). But while there needs to be fundamental continuity of this self over time, we also must account for change in the self. An essential way of accounting for those changes is by providing adequate causality, which Linde describes as providing convincing reasons for the change. All of this implies that our personal narrative is fluid and dynamic, never fixed. In order to achieve coherence, then, that narrative must constantly be reformulated (Hermans, 1997).

The reformulation of personal narratives has a social dimension, since they are shaped by the culture in which they are embedded and through which they are given meaning. Sarbin (1993) points out that we live in "a story-shaped world" (p. 63), surrounded as we are by narratives of all kinds—myths and folklore, popular television shows and movies, social scripts and mores, religious histories and parables—all of which embody our cultural values. These provide what Sarbin calls "libraries of plots . . . [that] help us interpret our own and other people's experience" (p.59). Linde (1993) speaks of a cultural supply of normal events, reasonable causes, and plausible explanations that are not only available to us in constructing our life stories but that also offer the legitimacy of normalcy. Personal narratives are also social because they require an audience, whether real or an imagined Other, or even the self. In that sense we can think of these stories as performances, played out in multiple ways but always referencing cultural norms.

Because of the connection between narrative and identity, stories offer enormous potential as a mode of personal change. Sometimes that change comes from identifying with a powerful story that makes sense of a person's experience in a new way. Alcoholics Anonymous, for example, provides a narrative of decline and degradation caused by alcoholism, which then becomes a narrative of restoration and new life through a structured process of behavioral and attitudinal change. I believe that the power of the story lies in the fact that alcoholics who have hit bottom can identify deeply with the first half of the story they hear at AA and, because they see others who were once like them now living a better life, can embrace the second half in the belief that their lives can change as well.

One type of narrative learning can occur through the process of therapy. While this is the underlying principle of Freudian psychoanalysis, it is a relatively new idea in psychotherapy, which has largely been shaped by the medical model of identifying problems and treating them. Narrative psychology focuses on the life story itself (Sarbin, 1986). Narratives, after all, are what clients bring to therapists; through the dialogic relationship between the therapist and the client, that narrative is reconstructed. This could involve bringing to the surface significant submerged themes within the narrative, or developing a narrative that is more coherent and unified (Polkinghorne, 1988). White and Epston (1990) focus on altering the plot form, for example, casting clients as heroes rather than victims in their stories. Josselson (1995, p. 33) speaks of this as "reframing a story in search of life plots that better serve the individual in the present." However these reconstructions proceed, the new narratives offer clients a more satisfying way of understanding themselves and of moving into the future. "Each analysis amounts in the end to retelling a life in the past and present—and as it may be in the future. A life is re-authored as it is co-authored" (Schafer, 1992, p. xv).

A similar process occurs when a person keeps a journal or diary, though here it is a dialogue of the self with the self and not with another person. There is a long history to journaling and it is probably the most accessible form of personal writing. I think that a large part of this popularity is connected to the privacy of the form—it is writing about the self, for the self. It's also a highly varied form whose structure is self-determined. Lukinsky (1990) sees it as a tool for introspection, powerful especially because it allows the person to withdraw from an experience in order to reflect on it, then reenter active life with a new or deeper understanding of that experience. Wiener and Rosenwald (1993), in their study of diarists, conclude that the form offers many psychological benefits, in part because "the diary is multifaceted as a 'space' and an 'object' (in the psychoanalytic sense of an other); as a process and a product; as a container, its contents, and the experience of containment" (p. 51). Among the benefits they found are the management of boundaries and emotions, and the exploration of aspects of the self (the so-called mirror function). Most significant, however, is the benefit of personal growth, or what Wiener and Rosenwald call "the mobilization of memory in the service of new living" (p. 53).

While there is no prescribed form for journals or diaries, the most well-known approach is probably Progoff's intensive journaling process. Progoff (1975) designed workshops on his method for adults who want to systematically examine their lives in order to develop a more complex understanding of themselves. He divides the journal into three sections: first, life history information, developed in multiple ways; then various dialogues with this information; and finally, a depth exploration of dreams, images, and other inner experiences as they relate to the previous two sections. These sections are not written in a linear way; instead, the journalist moves back and forth between sections, allowing each to inform the other. Progoff's approach, while not for everyone, is wonderfully creative and flexible, and engagement with it enables people to develop unexpected new insights about themselves.

Narrative, then, provides a very natural mode of learning, linked as it is to the meaning-making process. There are lots of ways this already is being used in educational settings. Learning journals, for example, can be used by learners to examine both the process and content of their learning (Kerka, 1996), and by teachers to reflect on the effectiveness of their teaching (Holt, 1994). Dominicé (2000) applies life history to learning by having students write their educational biography and thereby understand how learning has shaped who they are. Unlike somatic learning, narrative learning is something with which we're already familiar and comfortable. The challenge here is to expand our understanding of narrative and explore exactly how narrative can both facilitate and explain the learning process.

Conclusion

Adult learning happens, and some of it happens outside the boundaries that, at any particular moment, define adult education as a field. I hope that the two types of learning that I have briefly explored here will not only be of interest in themselves, but also encourage adult educators to look around and to notice new modes of learning. The prairie is wide, the rabbit trails are many, and it is always in the best interest of the continued growth of our field to explore them. Which ones would you choose?

References

Berman, M. *Coming to Our Senses: Body and Spirit in the Hidden History of the West.* New York: Simon & Schuster, 1989.

Bordo, S. R. *The Flight to Objectivity.* Albany, NY: SUNY Press, 1987.

Bruner, J. *Actual Minds, Possible Worlds.* Cambridge, MA: Harvard University Press, 1986.

Crowdes, M. S. "Embodying Sociological Imagination: Pedagogical Support for Linking Bodies to Minds." *Teaching Sociology,* 2000, *28,* 24–40.

Dominicé, P. F. *Learning from Our Lives: Using Educational Biographies with Adults.* San Francisco: Jossey-Bass, 2000.

Gergen, K. J., and Gergen, M. M. "Narrative and the Self as Relationship." *Advances in Experimental Social Psychology,* 1988, *21,* 17–56,

Hermans, H.J.M., "Self-Narrative in the Life Course: A Contextual Approach." In M. Bamberg (ed.), *Narrative Development: Six Approaches.* Mahwah, NJ: Lawrence Erlbaum, 1997.

Heshusius, L., and Ballard, K. *From Positivism to Interpretivism and Beyond.* New York: Teachers College Press, 1996.

Holt, S. "Reflective Journal Writing and Its Effects on Teaching Adults." In *The Year in Review,* vol. 3. Dayton, VA: Virginia Adult Educators Research Network, 1994. (ED 375 302)

Jaggar, A. M., and Bordo, S. R. *Gender/Body/Knowledge.* New Brunswick, NJ: Rutgers University Press, 1989.

Josselson, R. "Imagining the Real: Empathy, Narrative, and the Dialogic Self." In R. Josselson and A. Lieblich (eds.), *Interpreting Experience. The Narrative Study of Lives,* vol. 3. Thousand Oaks, CA: Sage, 1995.

Kerka, S. "Journal Writing and Adult Learning." *ERIC Digest,* no. 174, 1996. (ED 399 413)

Linde, C. *Life Stories.* New York: Oxford University Press, 1993.

Lukinsky, J. "Reflective Withdrawal Through Journal Writing." In J. Mezirow (ed.), *Fostering Critical Reflection in Adulthood.* San Francisco: Jossey-Bass, 1990.

Mairs, N. *Carnal Acts.* New York: HarperCollins, 1990.

Matthews, J. C. "Somatic Knowing and Education." *The Educational Forum,* 1998, *62,* 236–242.

Michelson, E. "Re-membering: The Return of the Body to Experiential Learning." *Studies in Continuing Education,* 1998, *20,* 217–233.

Polanyi, M. *Knowing and Being.* Chicago: University of Chicago Press, 1969.

Polkinghorne, D. E. *Narrative Knowing and the Human Sciences.* Albany, NY: SUNY Press, 1988.

Progoff, I. *At a Journal Workshop.* New York: Dialogue House Library, 1975.

Riessman, C. K. *Narrative Analysis.* Qualitative Research Methods Series, no. 30. Newbury Park, CA: Sage, 1993.

Rosenwald, G. C., and Ochberg, R. L. *Storied Lives.* New Haven, CT: Yale University Press, 1992.

Rossiter, M. "A Narrative Approach to Development: Implications for Adult Education." *Adult Education Quarterly,* 1999, *50*(1), 56–71.

Sarbin, T. R. (ed.). *Narrative Psychology: The Storied Nature of Human Conduct.* New York: Praeger, 1986.

Sarbin, T. R. "The Narrative as the Root Metaphor for Contextualism." In S. C. Hayes, C. J. Hayes, H. W. Reese, and T. R. Sarbin, (eds.) *Varieties of Scientific Contextualism.* Reno, NV: Context Press, 1993.

Schafer, R. *Retelling a Life: Narration and Dialogue in Psychoanalysis*. New York: Basic Books, 1992.

White, M., and Epston, D. *Narrative Means to Therapeutic Ends*. New York: Norton, 1990.

Wiener, W. J., and Rosenwald, G. C. "A Moment's Monument: The Psychology of Keeping a Diary." In R. Josselson and A. Lieblich, (eds.), *The Narrative Study of Lives*, vol. 1. Newbury Park, CA: Sage, 1993.

M. CAROLYN CLARK is associate professor of adult education at Texas A&M University.

10

This chapter summarizes the recent additions to the knowledge base of adult learning theory and concludes with some thoughts on how these contributions are expanding adult learning theory.

Something Old, Something New: Adult Learning Theory for the Twenty-First Century

Sharan B. Merriam

Traditional weddings in the United States require the bride to wear "something old, something new, something borrowed, and something blue." The old, the new, the borrowed, and something colorful all have value in a woman's transition into a new role and a new phase in life. This adage provides a nice metaphor for the state of adult learning theory as we move into the new century. We have some foundational theories and models that are being revised, and we have new ways of looking at adult learning, some of which have been borrowed from other disciplines and some of which are certainly colorful! In this chapter, I first summarize the "old" and the "new" learning theories, then discuss how these theories are expanding our understanding of the learner, the learning process, and the context of learning.

The Old and the New

It is quite a misnomer to label andragogy, self-directed learning, and transformational learning "old." Perhaps "foundational" or even "traditional" might be better. In any case, these three theories or models of adult learning are distinct in that each has been developed and promoted by adult educators interested in differentiating adult learning from the learning of children. They also represent efforts to professionalize the field of adult education. That is, from the middle of the twentieth century on, it was thought that to be a profession or a discipline adult education had to develop its own knowledge base, and that knowledge base had to be distinct and unique

New Directions for Adult and Continuing Education, no. 89, Spring 2001 © Jossey-Bass, A Publishing Unit of John Wiley & Sons, Inc.

from other areas of education. All three of these efforts became part of the literature base of adult learning in the 1970s.

Andragogy and self-directed learning, the focus of much research and scholarly discussions in the 1970s and 1980s, were eclipsed in the 1990s by transformational learning and other approaches to adult learning. Nevertheless, the past decade has seen additional scholarship in both areas. A lively international discussion is currently taking place as to whether andragogy is a science, a discipline, or a technology. A second stream of scholarship has been a critical and postmodern critique of the individual focus of andragogy; writers contend that the learner is always set in a socially-constructed context, a context that shapes the learning of the individual. Self-directed learning is also alive and well, though not as much research is taking place in this area compared to the mid-1980s. There is, however, more attention to theorizing, model-building, goals and ethics, and ways of assessing self-directed learning.

Anecdotal and testimonial reports have long supported the notion that people can be profoundly changed through learning. However, it wasn't until Freire's (1970) and more recently Mezirow's (1991, 2000) work in this area that transformational learning has achieved the status of a major theory of adult learning. In fact, the decade of the 1990s might be called the transformational learning decade in terms of its move to center stage as the focus of scholarly activity in adult learning. In Chapter Two, Lisa Baumgartner reviewed the very latest research on transformational learning.

The field of adult education has long realized that formal learning activities are just one mechanism for adult learning. Self-directed learning helped bring to the fore the importance of informal learning that occurs as we go about our daily lives. Our work life, our family life, and our community life are punctuated with incidences of informal and unplanned learning. Indeed, all life experiences are potentially learning experiences. Recently, organizations in particular have sought to document this kind of learning as a way of developing the learning organization. Victoria Marsick and Karen Watkins reviewed some of the definitions of, and research on, this somewhat elusive concept, and presented their model for understanding informal and incidental learning.

The center three chapters of this volume represent reformulations of three perspectives that were comparatively new additions when the 1993 *Update* was published. Each of these chapters draws from disciplines outside of adult education; hence, we are into the "borrowed" components of the mosaic of adult learning theory. Feminist theory and feminist pedagogy have greatly influenced adult educators' thinking about learning, and a chapter in the 1993 volume reflected this influence. Elisabeth Hayes's chapter on women learners in *this* volume advanced our understanding of learning by questioning some of the popular stereotypes associated with women learners, in particular that they learn best when in relationships with other learners and that they prefer affective and intuitive ways of knowing. Hayes then suggested that we view the learning situation as "gendered" and draw implications for practice accordingly.

Likewise, Catherine Hansman's chapter on context-based learning builds on the work in situated cognition. Coming from educational psychology, situated cognition posits that our knowing (cognition) is "situated" or resides in "authentic," real-life activity. The learning is shaped by the context; the tools or things in the setting that help us learn, like maps or computers; and the social interaction among people in the context. Communities of practice, a relatively new concept lodged in situated cognition theory, was presented in Hansman's chapter.

Critical theory and postmodernism are both "borrowed" from social theory. They are tools by which we can examine our assumptions and our practices in adult education. Deborah Kilgore in Chapter Six skillfully compared these two approaches and what they have to say about knowledge construction and power and how those critiques can illuminate our understanding of who, when, where, and what adults learn.

The last three chapters represent the "new" pieces in our adult learning mosaic. While philosophers, poets, psychologists, and others have thought about and written about emotions, consciousness, and somatic knowing, only recently have these topics been systematically explored in relation to learning. Although written independently of each other, these three chapters converge in interesting ways. John Dirkx suggested that significant learning in adult life has a strong emotional component, one that facilitates the meaning-making process. In reviewing recent research on the brain, Lilian Hill noted that emotions are embedded in neural networks, connecting the physical with the affective. Carolyn Clark came at this same connection from a slightly different angle in her discussion in Chapter Nine of somatic or embodied learning. Dirkx and Hill also pointed out the importance of the mind, imagination, and consciousness in the learning process, and that imagination has a role in storytelling, or narrative learning, as discussed in Clark's chapter.

In summary, andragogy, self-directed learning, and transformative learning theory are familiar pieces of the adult learning mosaic, as is informal and incidental learning. There are others being added to the picture, some borrowed from other disciplines, some very new. What is uncertain is whether any of these newer concepts, models, or theories will achieve the status of the earlier contributions. But perhaps that's not the question to ask. A more important consideration is how the newer approaches are expanding our understanding of adult learning.

Implications for Adult Learning Theory

As I stated in the Editor's Notes, I doubt that there will ever be a single theory of adult learning powerful enough to capture the complexity of this phenomenon. While a grand theory of adult learning might seem to make our task easier in explaining our field to others, it would have to be so broad it would ultimately explain nothing. A much more vibrant model is what we have now—a prism of theories, ideas, and frameworks that allows us to see the same phenomenon from different angles. Some of these angles are tried and true—andragogy and self-directed learning, for example. Some have just within the last decade become more prominent, such as transformational learning and informal and incidental learning. Other angles are borrowed and applied to our field, such as feminist pedagogy, situated cognition, and critical and postmodern theory. Yet other approaches having to do with emotions, consciousness, and the body are just now appearing in our literature.

There are at least three ways in which *all* of these approaches are contributing to our understanding of adult learning. First, the *adult learner* is seen wholistically. The learner is more than a cognitive machine processing information. He or she comes with a mind, memories, conscious and subconscious worlds, emotions, imagination, and a physical body, all of which can interact with new learning. Second, the *learning process* is much more than the systematic acquisition and storage of information. It is also making sense of our lives, transforming not just what we learn but the way we learn, and it is absorbing, imagining, intuiting, and learning informally with others. Finally, the *context* in which learning occurs has taken on greater importance. Not only can we see learning as situated in a particular context, but we can examine how race, class, gender, power and oppression, and conceptions of knowledge and truth shape the context in the first place and subsequently the learning that occurs. Indeed, as in the past, new developments in adult learning theory are contributing to a more comprehensive understanding of adult learning, an understanding that is both dynamic and changing.

References

Freire, P. *Pedagogy of the Oppressed.* New York: Seabury Press, 1970.
Mezirow, J. *Transformative Dimensions of Adult Learning.* San Francisco: Jossey-Bass, 1991.
Mezirow, J., and Associates. *Learning as Transformation: Rethinking Adult Learning and Development.* San Francisco: Jossey-Bass, 2000.

SHARAN B. MERRIAM is professor of adult education at The University of Georgia, Athens.

INDEX

Adult learning: ability, 4; aging effects on, 76–77; andragogy model, 4–8, 93–94; andragogy versus self-directed learning, 11; behavioral psychological perspective, 3–4; brain function and, 79–80; competence, defined, 56; connections between individual and social, 58; context-based, 43–49; critique of psychological focus of, 7; deconstruction of theories, 56; demands from business and industry, 44; dependency on teacher, 5; early research on, 3–4; expression of emotions in, 64–65; future for, 49, 95–96; imaginal method, 69–70; informal and incidental learning theory, 25–31, 94; informational learning, 16; importance of attending to emotions in, 68; and job performance, 56–57; learner-centered programming, 6; life experiences as barriers to, 5; models challenged by critical and postmodern theories, 53–60; motivation, 5; and narrative learning, 87–89; noncognitive factors influence on, 4; personal responsibility orientation (PRO) model, 9; role of emotions in, 63–64, 67–68; self-directed learning (SDL) model, 8–11; 93–94; shift from individual to group, 58; somatic learning, 84–87; speed of, 4; staged self-directed learning (SSDL) model, 9; textbooks, 55–56; transformational learning theory, 15–22, 93–94; using images to make sense of emotions in, 68–70. *See also* Context-based adult learning
African American women, 39–40
Aging: brain changes in, 76–77
Ahmed, M., 26
Alcoholics Anonymous, 88
Alvarez, A., 45
Amey, M., 64
Andragogy: continuum with pedagogy, 6; criticism of theory, 5; defined by learning situation, 6; definition, 4–5; European and American conceptions of, 7; German origin of term, 6–7; importance of theory, 93–95; Knowle's program, 5; planning model, 5; as sci-

entific discipline, 6; as technological application of knowledge, 6; as theory versus model, 5; underlying assumptions, 5
Andruske, C. L., 9
Argyris, C., 26, 28
Avis, J., 57

Bagnall, R. G., 56
Ballard, K., 84, 86
Bandura, A., 26
Baudelot, C., 58
Baumgartner, L. M., 21, 94
Belenky, M. F., 35, 37
Berman, M., 84
Blum, D., 74
Bonk, J. B., 44, 49
Bordo, S. R., 84, 85
Boud, D., 26, 68
Bourdieu, P., 58
Brain: and adult learning, 79–80; aging effects on, 76–77; changes and reorganization of, 74–75; embryonic development of, 73; and emotions and learning, 76; environmental influences on, 74; gender differences in, 74; hormonal influence on, 74; and learning and memory, 75, 76; and the mind and consciousness, 77–78; neurobiology of, 73–77; structure and functions of, 74
Brazil: transformational learning studies in, 16
Bregman, E. O., 3
Brockett, R. B., 9, 10
Brookfield, S., 9, 55, 68
Brown, J., 44, 45, 46, 48, 49
Bruner, J., 87
Bryant, I., 55, 56, 57
Buckmaster, A., 46, 47
Buncombe, M., 77
Business incubators, 26–27

Caffarella, R. S., 4, 8, 9, 10, 45, 57, 68
Callahan, M. H. W., 26, 27
Campbell, S., 67
Candy, P. C., 10, 26
Cardillichio, T., 75

Back Issue/Subscription Order Form

Copy or detach and send to:
Jossey-Bass, 350 Sansome Street, San Francisco CA 94104-1342

Call or fax toll free!
Phone 888-378-2537 6AM-5PM PST; Fax 800-605-2665

Back issues: Please send me the following issues at $27 each.
(Important: please include series initials and issue number, such as ACE78.)

1. ACE _____

_____

_____

$ _____ Total for single issues

$ _____ Shipping charges (for single issues ***only;*** subscriptions are exempt from shipping charges): Up to $30, add $5^{50} • $30^{01}–$50, add $6^{50} $50^{01}–$75, add $8 • $75^{01}–$100, add $10 • $100^{01}–$150, add $12 Over $150, call for shipping charge.

Subscriptions Please ❏ start ❏ renew my subscription to *New Directions for Adult and Continuing Education* for the year _____ at the following rate:

U.S.:	❏ Individual $59	❏ Institutional $114
Canada/Mexico:	❏ Individual $59	❏ Institutional Canada $154
All Others:	❏ Individual $83	❏ Institutional $188

NOTE: Subscriptions are quarterly, and are for the calendar year only. Subscriptions begin with the Spring issue of the year indicated above. Prices are subject to change.

$ _____ Total single issues and subscriptions (Add appropriate sales tax for your state for single issues. No sales tax on U.S. subscriptions. Canadian residents, add GST for subscriptions and single issues.)

❏ Payment enclosed (U.S. check or money order only)

❏ VISA, MC, AmEx, Discover Card #_____ Exp. date_____

Signature _____ Day phone _____

❏ Bill me (U.S. institutional orders only. Purchase order required.)

Purchase order #_____

Federal Tax I.D. 135593032   GST 89102-8052

Name _____

Address _____

_____

Phone_____ E-mail _____

For more information about Jossey-Bass, visit our Web site at:
www.josseybass.com   **PRIORITY CODE = ND1**